With sincere thanks & best wishes

Dec '79

[illegible]

OLD SHEFFIELD TOWN

A NEW

REVISED EDITION

OLD SHEFFIELD TOWN
AN HISTORICAL MISCELLANY

J. EDWARD VICKERS

APPLEBAUM BOOKSHOP LIMITED

First published by EP Publishers
Limited, Wakefield, 1972
Updated and revised edition by
Applebaum Limited 1979

TO MY WIFE,
RUBY

Photoset, printed and bound
in Great Britain by
REDWOOD BURN LIMITED
Trowbridge & Esher

AUTHOR'S NOTE

First published in 1972, this popular book has been revised and the contents slightly altered in order not only to bring the information up to date, but also to make this a complement to my 'Popular History of Sheffield', published in June this year.

Though a number of the historic buildings included in Part 1 have now been demolished, I have again included these as I consider it is as important to know what we have lost as well as what still remains. I have also included at the end of Part 1 a few notes on other past and present buildings which were not mentioned in the 1972 edition.

Part 2 'Sheffield's Ancient Suburbs' is reprinted without alteration.

Part 3 has many new features and now includes tales, anecdotes and legends which I have added to the 'Story of Old Sheffield' printed in the original edition.

My object has been to make this revised edition of 'Old Sheffield Town' a truly informative and entertaining book

J. Edward Vickers
Sheffield, November, 1978.

FOREWORD

by Professor G.R. Potter, C.B.E., M.A., PH.D., F.S.A., F.R.HIST.S.

Any one who is interested in the continuing story of a great city will welcome this complete revision of an earlier and most attractive book from Mr. J. Edward Vickers. He has devoted many years to the study of old Sheffield, and with great skill succeeds in showing the unbroken connection between the old and the new, for he never loses sight of the interests of those now enjoying the fruit of the labours of their forefathers.

He has cast his net widely to bring into his narrative of Sheffield those outlying parts which a century ago were thought of as separate and are now happily integrated into what has become a metropolitan district.

To this he has added a store of legends and anecdotes which will bring extra enjoyment to the many readers to whom this volume is addressed.

George Potter,
Herongate,
Derwent Lane,
Hathersage.

December, 1978.

CONTENTS

PART 1
THE OLD & HISTORIC BUILDINGS OF SHEFFIELD

ILLUSTRATIONS

Except where acknowledged, all
illustrations are from the
author's collection

PART 1
THE OLD & HISTORIC BUILDINGS OF SHEFFIELD

'It is a sin and a disgrace
That many buildings, fair of face,
Have been demolished, bulldozed down
And lost forever to Sheffield Town'

The Cathedral Church of SS. Peter and Paul

How long a church has stood on the site of the Cathedral we are unable to say, but we know that the present church was founded by the first William de Lovetot, a Norman, in the time of Henry I (1100–1135). Before this time there may have been a small wooden church, for a Saxon Cross was erected on this site sometime before the year 825. This Cross was removed by order of Queen Elizabeth I and is now housed in the British Museum.

An old chronicler states that early in the 12th century, Sheffield possessed 'a church, a corn mill, an hospital, a bridge, and a castle for its protection'.

However, in 1266, during the Civil War, when the barons were in arms against King Henry III, John d'Eyville on his march towards Chesterfield, sacked and burnt the town, including the castle and the church. The church was rebuilt some years later, by another Norman, Thomas de Furnival and in 1280, Archbishop Wickwane dedicated the Church of SS. Peter and Paul in Sheffield.

The earliest recorded institution of a vicar was in 1308, this gentleman's name being John de Twistleton.

Just after the year 1520, George, the Fourth Earl of Shrewsbury, erected for himself and his descendants, the Shrewsbury Chapel (now the Sanctuary of the Lady Chapel), at the south-east corner of the church. Anne, his first wife, who died in 1520, was buried here. In 1538, George died, and his fine alabaster tomb, which is situated under the flat topped arch between the High Sanctuary and the Lady Chapel, shows the Fourth Earl in his robes of the Garter. Anne, his first wife, is on one side of him, while Elizabeth, his second wife, is on the other.

In 1556 the Parish Registers were commenced, in which all

baptisms, marriages and deaths were recorded.

George, the Sixth Earl of Shrewsbury, died in 1590, and his large memorial can be seen against the south wall of the Lady Chapel. This memorial, erected by the Earl before his death, shows his effigy in armour, the head on a rolled up end of a straw mat. There is a large architectural surround over the figure. The Sixth Earl is famous as the custodian for fifteen years of Mary, Queen of Scots, during her imprisonment in Sheffield. Also the Earl's second wife was Bess of Hardwick, who built the marvellous Hardwick Hall. Altogether 18 members of the Shrewsbury family are interred in the vaults below the chapel.

In the year 1650, the Puritans, who disliked music in the churches, silenced the organ, which had played for many years above the Rood Loft. The earliest reference to this instrument seems to be in the will of John Wickersley, dated 24th April, 1528, This directed that his executors should 'cause the loft in the Roode chapell, wher th' organnes now standes, to be new buylded'.

The Church was now called the Trinity Church, and continued to be so called right up to the opening of the 19th century.

The cruciform outline of the church was finally obliterated in 1777, when a vestry, with a room above for the Church Burgesses, was erected on the north side of the chancel.

Between 1790 and 1805 great changes were made, the entire nave being rebuilt, galleries erected and pews fixed to the ground floor. However, the queerest alteration during this time, was the filling in, with brickwork, of all the arches of the chancel and aisles. Only a small door was left between the nave and the chancel. The organ and a three-decker pulpit stood beneath the tower and there were deep galleries on the other three sides.

In 1857 the organ was moved to the shallow transept then existing to the north of the tower before the North Transept was built in 1880. Also the central archway was cleared of all the obstructions, so that the chancel became open to the body of the church.

Between the years 1878 to 1880 vast alterations and restorations were carried out. All the ugly brickwork was removed, the galleries were taken down and the North and South Transepts were built. The nave was lengthened, a west porch added and the ground floor was reseated with oak benches. Also a room for the Church Burgesses was built on the north side, with vestries for the clergy and choir. £21,000 was expended on this transformation of the church, plus large sums for memorial windows and other gifts.

A fine example of the carver's art, a beautiful oak reredos (the structure behind and above the altar) was set up in the chancel in 1885. A curious inscription on the back of this reredos read 'Harry

The Cathedral

Bellwood Photography Ltd

Hems and his merrie men made this reredos at Exeter AD 1885. However, a new reredos, a gift of the Freemasons, was erected in 1920 and Harry Hems' work was removed. The reredos given by the Freemasons is now to be seen in the Chapel of the Holy Spirit.

In 1933 the Duke of Norfolk relinquished the Shrewsbury Chapel which, up to that time, had been the private chapel of the Shrewsbury family and this enabled much restoration work to be accomplished. An unused tomb which had been occupying a centre position in the Chapel was removed and this can now be seen in the churchyard on the north side of the Cathedral.

Certain extensions to the Cathedral were begun in 1937 and a foundationstone was laid by the Princess Royal. Also work was begun on the Chapter House, a gift of Miss F.L. Tozer, in memory of her father and mother. The first part of the extensions and the Chapter House were completed in 1939, but before the second stage could be commenced the Second World War broke out. Unfortunately the war made it necessary for a large modification of the original enlargement plans and eventually the architect, Mr. Arthur Bailey, prepared the plans of the Cathedral as we see it today.

The new building was begun in June, 1963 and was completed during the late summer of 1966. On the 15th November of that year, Princess Margaret attended the re-hallowing of the West End of the nave and the consecration of the restored Chapel of St. George.

For the West End, Derbyshire stone, quarried at Darly Dale, was used and the entrance is through full length glass doors, trimmed with stainless steel.

The interior now gives an impression of great spaciousness, the main structure being supported by four fifty-foot high columns. Though appearing to be of sandstone, these are, in fact, blocks of pre-cast concrete faced with stone dust.

Set fifty feet up in the roof is a lantern of wood and glass, which in sunlight throws beautiful patterns onto the floor and walls. The ornamental woodwork surrounding the lantern is a representation of the thorns of the crucifixion.

In the north wall, facing the entrance, is a large stained glass window, erected to the memory of Edward Birks, which was formerly in the wall of the old west end.

Other new sections of the Cathedral include the interesting St. George's Chapel, in which can be seen, amongst many proud but tattered colours, the ensign of H.M.S. Sheffield; while to the north of St. George's Chapel is the beautiful Chapel of the Holy Spirit.

Architecture

To return to the earlier architecture of the Cathedral, very little of the present structure appears to be of a date before the 15th century. The chancel, the north aisle and portions of the tower are the only parts of the mediaeval architecture still remaining. However, some of the stones from the early Norman church can still be seen embodied in the masonry of the east wall.

One of the reasons why so little of the early church is left, is that from the reign of Elizabeth I, the nave of the church gradually fell into decay. In fact, the church became so dilapidated that at the end ofthe 18th century, the Twelve Capital Burgesses stated that 'the Parish Church of Sheffield has become ruinous and in decay in the walls, arches, pews, roofs and other parts of the fabric all need immediate reparation and amendment'.

It was therefore decided to pull down the old 15th century nave and a new one was built and reopened on 6th October, 1805.

Church Treasures

Two of the most valuable treasures of the Cathedral are a portable sedilia and a Jesse window.

The sedilia (or seats for the priests) is to be found in the Chapel of St. Katherine against the wall of the Sanctury. This carved, black oak, portable sedilia is probably 15th century work and is extremely rare.

The Jesse window is situated in the north wall of the aisle at the west end of the transept. This window of ancient glass, is probably the work of Spanish artists of the 14th century and was brought to the Cathedral in 1946 from St. Luke's Church in Hollis Croft. The brilliance of some of the colours, especially the blues, is particularly noticeable.

On the north wall of the High Sanctuary is a bust of the Rev. James Wilkinson, of particular interest because this was the first work in marble executed by Sir Francis Chantrey,Sheffield's famous sculptor.

Other furnishings of interest in the Church are the Font, a gift of the Freemasons in 1881; the brass eagle Lectern, presented by Benjamin Shepherd in 1883 and the richly carved pulpit, the gift of Mrs. Wilson of Banner Cross.

The earliest memorial in the Cathedral, still in existence today, is a brass bearing the following inscription:

> 'Here lyeth Elizabeth, doughter of Thomas,
> Erle of Ormonde, and of Lore his wyf,
> Somtyme wyf to the Lorde Mountioye, Which
> Elizabeth deceased the XX day of ffebruary
> the yere of our Lord MCCCCX (1410), on whose
> soule jhu have mercy men (Amen).'

Of interest to the architectural historian is a Mass Clock or Scratch Dial, which can be seen on the south wall of the Lady Chapel. This was probably brought in from an outside wall during the rebuilding of the 15th century church.

Practically all the painted glass windows depicting historical events are of recent origin and one of the most noticeable is situated in the east wall of the transept. This window, of 1938, to the memory of Bernard Alexander Firth, was created by Christopher Webb, and shows six figures, all outstanding personages of Sheffield's history. These are Waltheof, William de Lovetot, Gerard de Furnival, Thomas Nevil, John Talbot and John Bright.

Chapter House Glass

The other historically interesting windows are all in the 1939 Chapter House and, commencing at the west end of the north wall, show various events in Sheffield history, as briefly follows: William de Lovetot building from the Norman Church about 1101; the Monks of Kirkstead Abbey smelting iron at Kimberworth about 1161; Thomas de Furnival presenting a Charter of Rights and Privileges to his Free Tenants in 1297; Wickwane, Archbishop of York, dedicating the Early English Church about 1280; Cardinal Wolsey at the Manor Lodge in 1530; Sir Thomas de Chaworth granting the right to mine coal to the Canons of Beauchief about 1310; Mary, Queen of Scots, at the Manor Lodge with her secretary, Pierre Rollet in 1569; Queen Mary granting a Charter to the Twelve Capital Burgesses in 1554; the ejection of James Fisher under the Act of Uniformity in 1662; Benjamin Huntsman inventing Crucible Steel about 1742; William Elles, the first Cutler to be granted a private mark for his knives in 1554; John Wesley preaching in Paradise Square in 1779; Leonard Hedley placing the Cross on the Chapel of St. George in 1938; Robert Sanderson at school in Rotherham in 1600; and finally a window showing Chaucer's Canterbury Pilgrims, commemorating the line from 'Canterbury Tales', 'A Sheffield thwitel (Knife) baar he in his hose (trousers)'.

A small light high up in the eastern wall, shows the Sheffield Cross, a typical specimen of 9th century Mercian craftmanship. The shaft of this Anglo-Saxon Cross is now exhibited in the Iron Age Gallery of the British Museum, but was up to 1942, an ornament in Mrs. G.M. Staniforth's private garden in Sheffield.

The Churchyard

The churchyard was originally much larger than it is today. Up to 1758, Church Street, then known as 'Church Lane', was very narrow, with the upper stories of the wooden buildings projecting over the road. However, it was widened in 1785, 1866 and again in 1891, each time causing a little of the churchyard to disappear. The churchyard has been used for many things, including a playground for the boys at the Charity School at the corner of East Parade and as a fairground on the day of the annual Cutlers' Feast.

No burials took place after 1855 and all the gravestones have now been laid flat to form paving stones.

The Charity Schools

On the north, east and west of the Cathedral are the buildings of Georgian Sheffield.

In St. James Row, which incidentally was called 'Virgin's Row' in the 18th century (to the west of the Cathedral) is the former Girls' Charity School of 1786. This is a brick building of five bays with three bay pediment. The school was used to 'educate, maintain, clothe and train' sixty girls in preparation for domestic service.

The other buildings in St. James Row are not very impressive, but more rewarding structures are to be found opposite in East Parade, which is situated at the east end of the churchyard.

Here can be seen the Boys' Charity School, a stone faced, three storied building in the classical style. Rebuilt in 1825, this building replaced the original Charity School of 1710. Designed to give education to one hundred poor boys of the town, the school existed for many years, until it was eventually transferred to premises in Psalter Lane. The former school is now in use as offices.

Other buildings of interest in East Parade, are No. 10, which is Gothic in appearance and No. 12 which has a pleasant Georgian doorcase, considered to be one of the most pleasing in the city centre.

Old Banker's House

Bellwood Photography Ltd.

The Old Banker's House

At the north end of the churchyard, No. 3 Hartshead is a most interesting structure. This is Broadbent House, usually called 'The Old Banker's House'. It is a brick building of five bays and three storeys with rusticated giant pilasters flanking the middle bay.

The house was built in 1728 and this date can still be seen, together with the initials N.R.B. on the rainwater head at the front of the building. The initials are those of Nicholas and Rebecca Broadbent and it was in this house that one of the earlier private banks of Sheffield was established. Its founder was Thomas Broadbent, a grandson of Nicholas and the bank commenced business in 1771. It was this same Thomas who was responsible for the greater number of houses in Paradise Square and in his later years, for Page Hall, which he commenced to build for his own use. However he was unable to complete this large house, for in 1782 his banking business collapsed.

It is said that Broadbent closed the bank doors on Saturday knowing full well that he was ruined and that he would not be able to open for business on the following Monday. But he said nothing to his customers and when one called on the Sunday and wished to do business he was bluntly told that none was conducted on that day. However when it became clear that the man only wished to make a deposit, Broadbent accepted the business!

In St. Peter's Close is a bricked up doorway which was probably the entrance to the bank and it is most likely that this was the door that was closed and locked when the bank failed in 1782. After his bankruptcy Broadbent is described as 'moving about, a pathetic object, bearing all the symbols of extreme poverty'. The house was later occupied by a merchant called Turner, who was followed by the Binneys, merchants and steel melters.

Originally this old house stood by itself in large grounds, with an avenue leading to it from York Street. Before St. Peter's Close waş built all this area were the gardens belonging to the house.

There are a number of vaulted cellars beneath the building, some of them twenty feet below the level of the road. Some of the rooms on the first and second floors are panelled in pine wood, have fine fireplaces and also ceilings of modelled plaster.

In the front attic, at one time, was a crane and it is still possible to see the winding post, connected between two beams, reaching from floor to ceiling. A silent reminder of the old merchant trading days.

The present owners of this interesting Old Banker's House, are Fuller Peiser, a firm of Chartered Surveyors.

Leader House

Just before 1760, Thomas Leader, a fine silversmith, left his home in Essex and came to Sheffield. With Henry Tudor he founded, in 1762, the firm of Tudor, Leader & Co. Silver Platers, whose speciality were beautiful snuff boxes.

In 1777 Thomas Leader leased from the Duke of Norfolk, the house that was to carry his name to the present day.

Unfortunately a new street plan of 1780 spoilt the garden on the west side and Thomas Leader, son of the above Thomas, subsequently leased a plot extending on the other side of the house.

His son, the third Thomas Leader, eloped with Miss Sarah Henfrey, who was the daughter of John Henfrey, Master Cutler in 1792, and they were married at Gretna Green on 7th December, 1791. This Thomas was also a Lieut. Colonel of the Sheffield Volunteer Infantry.

The house was altered sometime after 1788 by the addition of a bow window on the north front and the back premises were considerably changed.

Daniel Leader, who was the son of the first Thomas, also lived at Leader House. His son, Robert, in 1830, became a newspaper proprietor, and produced the 'Sheffield Independent', forerunner of what is now the 'Morning Telegraph.'

In 1817 Leader House was sold to the Pearson family, a daughter of the Pearsons marrying the brother of John Fowler, the designer of the Forth Bridge.

In 1853, Mr Pearson's daughter by his first wife, married H. Brown Fisher, a surgeon, and they resided at Leader House. The Fishers sold the house in 1872 to Charles Wardlow and he bequeathed it to his son, Marmaduke Wardlow. This gentleman spent a large sum restoring the property.

The house then passed through a number of hands, eventually becoming the property of the Sheffield Corporation in May, 1938.

On 20th March, 1970, the Corporation applied to the Minister of Housing for Listed Building Consent to demolish Leader House, so that the site could be used for the erection of a modern circular Register Office. This proposal was objected to by the Hallamshire Historic Building Society, a society of which the author is a founder member, and which was formed to prevent to wholesale destruction of Hallamshires' historic buildings. Because of the objection a Public Enquiry was held on 15th September, 1970. On 27th November, 1970, the Minister gave his decision that the house should not be demolished.

So Leader House, which is used by the Sheffield Polytechnic, still stands proudly, with its fine Georgian facade overlooking the busy, modern motor road, Arundel Gate.

Victoria Chambers

Adjacent to Hartshead is Fig Tree Lane, formerly a good example of one of the narrow, cobbled streets of ancient Sheffield. It is said that the name derives from a fig tree that grew in one of the gardens hereabouts.

On the right hand side as we proceed down the lane is a handsome structure known as 'Victoria Chambers'. Here a Dr. Aveling, with the co-operation of two other doctors, Jackson and Keeling founded the first 'Sheffield Hospital for Women'. It was opened in 1864 and was equipped with 6 beds, which were soon fully used. In 1865 three extra beds were provided, but even with these the small hospital could not cope with the demand.

By 1875 the hospital had become quite inadequate, so Thomas Jessop, owner of a large Sheffield steelworks, bought land at Leavygreave and built the Jessop Hospital for Women.

The south front of 'Victoria Chambers' has giant Ionic pilasters and the doorway in Fig Tree Lane has an Ionic porch. There is a fine circular staircase inside the building.

All the other houses of the 18th century which adjoined 'Victoria Chambers' have now been demolished to make way for a large modern brick office block, known as St. Peter's House.

Queen Street Chapel

Not very far from the bottom of Fig Tree Lane was Queen Street Chapel, one of the old brick built chapels of Sheffield.

The chapel arose because of a disagreement in 1782, between some of the older members of Nether Chapel, in Norfolk Street, and the Minister, the Rev. John Harmer.

Queen Street Chapel 1972

An approach was therefore made to the Church Burgesses for a building site and on 28th March, 1783, the Burgesses leased 'a piece of ground (then Wade's orchard) situate in a new street which was to be made and called either Fig Street or Queen Street, for the term of 99 years, at one penny halfpenny per yard, for the purpose of erecting a place of worship thereon'.

The Chapel was completed in 1784 and the first minister was Jehoiada Brewer, who came to Sheffield from the Congregational Church at Rodborough, in Gloucestershire. Mr Brewer accepted the call in March, 1783 and preached for the first time at the Chapel in Queen Street on 3rd December, 1783, even though, at that time, the chapel was only partly built. He remained Minister at the Chapel until the year 1796.

There is no plan or specification of the original building, but it is known that when first built the Chapel was 'fronted with a dead brick wall, no porch over the doors, all within as plain as the simplest whitewash, a narrow vestry at the lower end'.

The Chapel was enlarged in 1853–4 and in 1880–1 more extensive alterations were carried out at a cost of £5,000. New schools and vestries were built and the building as we knew it in 1967 was completed.

In the 18th century membership of the Chapel was taken very seriously, for we find that in 1794, the members pledged themselves to punctuality and regular attendance. One member, during this time, was suspended for a month for using 'unadvised words to his wife', whilst others were 'separated from membership for falsehood'.

Many noted Sheffield people worshipped at Queen Street Chapel, one of the most prominent being the poet, James Montgomery. When the Sunday School Union was founded at the Chapel in 1812, Montgomery was elected the first Sunday School President. At this time, the Sunday School, which was formed in 1806, had 640 scholars.

Unfortunately, owing to dwindling attendances, the old Chapel had to close its doors and the last service was held in January, 1967. The wheel has now turned full circle, for the remaining members have now rejoined the Nether Chapel (Now the Central United Reformed Church) from which they broke away 190 years ago.

Paradise Square

Situated between Queen Street and Campo Lane is Paradise Square, the old meeting place of the town.

Paradise Square *Bellwood Photography Ltd.*

Before the house we see today were built, the square was a cornfield called Hick's Stile Field. Pedestrians coming from the direction of West Bar, would travel up Silver Hill Head, cross the field diagonally by the narrow path, climb over Hick's Stile, then walk up Virgin's Row (now St. James Row) and cross the Churchyard to the town centre.

In 1736, Thomas Broadbent, of the Old Banker's House, took a lease of the field from the owners, the Trustees of Shrewsbury Hospital and he built the houses on the east side of the square. In 1771 further houses were erected and soon the square took on the appearance of the present day.

Being built upon a slope, it made an ideal place for public meetings and quite a number of famous people have spoken there. The rostrum used was the top of some steps which led to the first floor of a building on the north side of the Square. These steps have now disappeared, but the small balcony to which they led still remains. The building has had many uses, being at various times a Masonic Lodge, a private school and later shops and offices. It is now used as offices by the firm of D. Balfour & Sons, Consulting Engineers.

A plaque on one of the houses on the south side tells us that John Wesley, the noted preacher of the 18th century, held a meeting here, preaching to the largest congregation he ever saw on a weekday.

On market days, pots and pans, among other things, were sold in the Square and this led to its local name of 'Pot Square'.

In the centre were the town stocks, which were fixed there when they were moved from their original position near the south-west corner of the Churchyard. The last use of the stocks were for drunken men, these 'merry' citizens being placed there on Sundays, so that everyone had a chance of seeing them. However, over the years, the wooden stocks deteriorated, eventually they were taken into a yard at the rear of one of the houses and in the course of time they disappeared.

Sir Frances Chantrey, in the early part of his career, rented a room in the north-west corner of Paradise Square, where he painted portraits of many people of Sheffield for a few shillings. A plaque on the house informs us that Chantrey had a studio in that building in 1802.

A further plaque on the east side of the Square informs us that Dr. David Daniel Davis, a famous physician, lived in that particular house. Dr. Davis had the distinction of attending the birth of Queen Victoria in 1819.

In 1796, John Lees, a steel burner, sold his wife by public auction to Samuel Hill for sixpence! The poor wife was driven to the Square like a horse with a halter round her neck. This method of getting rid of an unwanted wife was quite popular around that time.

Paradise Square has altered little over the years and the houses built in 1736 and 1771 still look similar to what they must have looked to the people of Sheffield when they crowded there for their meetings, or buying and selling, in the 18th and 19th centuries.

It is advisable to visit this ancient part of the town on a Sunday for the best effect. On other days of the week, the cobbled centre of the Square is completely covered by the wholesale parking of motor vehicles.

The Queen's Head Hotel

On the other side of the town centre, poorly situated in Pond Hill between the Bus Station and grimy industrial buildings, is the oldest domestic building in Sheffield, the Queen's Head Hotel.

Formerly known as 'The Hawle (Hall) in the Ponds', the earliest mention of this interesting old house was in 1582 in an 'inventory of contents' made for George, the Six Earl of Shrewsbury.

Queen's Head Hotel 1972

It is considered by some to have been at one time the old laundry of Sheffield Castle, for in an extract from an account book in the Duke of Norfolk's Estate Office dated 17th July, 1770, it is referred to as 'an old house in the Ponds, formerly the wash-house to Sheffield Manor'. Also, it was recorded by Fairbanks in 1820 as the 'Mary, Queen of Scots, Wash House'.

When it was first built the hall was much larger than it is at present and we do know that the front gable was set back about five feet when the road was widened in the middle of the 19th century.

In 1949 the Smith Tadcaster Brewery Company Ltd. made extensive alterations to the interior and also renovated the exterior, which at that time was in a very bad state of neglect. All the main timbers had been covered over with planks of deal and the spaces between plastered over. The carved heads on the exterior had so many coats of whitewash on them that it was impossible to distinguish the features.

During the alterations to the interior of the building several interesting features were discovered, some of which had lain hidden and forgotten for many years. These included two tiny mullioned windows in a timber and plaster partition wall which faced the foot of the staircase and an interesting stone fireplace, which was found behind a cast-iron gate.

The stone fireplace, which is probably of the same date as the original house, is in the room on the right of the main entrance from Pond Hill.

Also, during the excavations for a new cellar, the workmen came upon a circular wall shaft and in a chimney were found two old clay pipes.

When the interior alterations had been completed, work was begun on the outside walls and the deal boards were removed revealing the original main timbers. Luckily it was found that these were in sufficiently good condition to be left exposed, enabling the spaces between to be replastered.

The carved heads were then stripped of the one eighth of an inch of whitewash which covered them and certain traces of paint were found. However these were so slight that it was not possible to preserve them.

A further interesting find was a strip of carved scroll work extending over the two windows on the ground floor. This was cleaned and left in its original position.

None of the windows are original, the ones on the first floor dating back to the middle of the 18th century and the ground floor windows are quite modern.

It is probable that the hotel took its name from the wooden

crowned female head on the west wall, but it must be remembered that 'Queen's Head' was a common name for inns and there were other houses of that name in Sheffield.

Viewing this ancient Tudor Hall, one must remember that when it was built it stood in very beautiful surroundings, open fields stretching towards the castle and large ponds, from which Pond Street takes its name, at the rearside.

Interesting Old Buildings in other parts of Sheffield

The following buildings when erected, were mostly in little villages that surrounded the town of Sheffield and to get to them often necessitated a long and uncomfortable journey. Today the ones that survive are part of the city and distance is no object owing to modern roads and transport.

Carlton House

Carlton House formerly stood in Kimberley Street, just off the main Attercliffe Road. Built just before 1771, it was situated in a large pleasure ground, about an acre and a half in extent, and had a beautiful garden and a pond. A winding drive commenced where Kimberley Street now begins and led down to the house.

At that time the property belonged to George Greave, but in 1819 the house was left to Thomas Howard. In the early 1840's Samuel Jackson, of the firm Spear and Jackson, lived there, but later the house became the residence of Thomas Sherhon, who was a physician and surgeon.

In 1840 Kimberley Street was constructed, taking the place of the old carriage drive.

From the year 1960 all Attercliffe deteriorated, houses and shops being closed & then demolished. Carlton House, which had been used for many years as doctors' surgeries also deteriorated with the surrounding property, until it was eventually destroyed with the buildings around.

Hill Top Chapel

Still situated in Hill Top Cemetary, near Attercliffe Road, is the small historic Hill Top Chapel.

This stone Gothic building was erected in 1629 as a Chapel of Ease to the Sheffield Parish Church (now the Cathedral).

Hill Top Chapel

Bellwood Photography Ltd.

The decision to build a chapel at Attercliffe was made by the principal inhabitants of that district and two stonemasons, Thomas Arnalde and Henry Barber were engaged to build the walls. The initials of these workmen, with the date 1629, can still be seen carved in the stone over the small northern doorway. Thomas Hicks, a carpenter, then constructed the roofing and John Wilson was chosen to receive the people's free will offerings and to pay the workmen's wages.

The Chapel was opened on 10th October, 1630, the first sermon being preached by the Rev. Thomas Toller. The consecration of the Chapel took place six years later, on the 26th October, 1636.

In 1648, William Bagshawe, the Apostle of the Peak, then 21 years old, became the minister and he remained at Attercliffe until 1651, when he vacated the ministry to return to his native Glossop.

When the Hill Top Chapel was first built it was much larger than the one we see today, being 66 feet long by 30 feet wide. The chapel was built mostly with the aid of Stephen and John Bright of Carbrook Hall and it is recorded that 'Mr. Bright procured a bell, and beautified the quier with sentances of scripture at his own charge'. The cost of building the chapel was £109 and the price of the land was £3:8s:0d.

At the west end a small gallery served for the musicians of the time, men who with wood wind and stringed instruments provided more or less harmony for the old style tunes sung to the psalms. Later, it is recorded, a barrel organ was installed and after that, a manual organ played by an organist who, oddly enough, was minus a finger on each hand.

It appears that some of the wealthier members of the chapel, the Fulls and Milners, erected a gallery at the north side and pocketed the rents for the pews for about forty years.

Unfortunately, in the eighteen hundreds, the Chapel fell into disuse and in the Attercliffe Almanack of 1895 we read, 'As we enter the damp old chapel we are struck by the absence of all attempts to maintain the place in repair. Windows evidently broken by the stone throwing urchins of these degenerate days. . . .'

In 1897 the Chapel was altered to its present size, but it was not until 1909 that it was properly restored and rededicated for divine service.

Now the Hill Top Chapel is in a worse state than in 1895, the windows are gone and boarded up and there is nothing of the interior except rubble. The stone work of the exterior is gradually crumbling and unless some effort is made in the near future to restore the building, the chapel will be no more.

At either side of the chapel door, at the front, were the memorial tablets to the memory of Rachel, mother of the Rev. Edward Goodwin, who died in 1787, and Elizabeth, who died in 1786, wife of the Rev. Goodwin. Only one of these tablets now remain and it is impossible to read the inscription owing to the weathering of the stone.

In the small cemetery that surrounds the Chapel most of the families of early Attercliffe were buried, among them the Swallows of New Hall, the Machins of the steel trade, the Staniforths of Darnall, many members of the Sorby family and Benjamin Huntsman, the inventor of crucible steel.

The Britannia Inn

In Worksop Road, just off Attercliffe Road, stands the Britannia Inn, not a very prepossessing building architecturally, but very interesting because of its connection with Benjamin Huntsman.

There is no definite date when the inn was built, but it was probably in the late 17th or early 18th century. It was formally two dwelling houses and the residence of Benjamin Huntsman when he had his works in Church Street (now Worksop Road) in 1772.

It was about this time when the date 1772 in large metal (probably steel) numbers were affixed to the gable end of the house.

In 1819 it is recorded that the two houses belonged to Ann Hancock, a widow, and they were occupied by her and her brother Benjamin. With the two houses were a workshop, warehouse and yard. Here Charles and Benjamin Hancock had carried on their business of fender makes and manufacturers of several kinds of knives.

During the years that followed these two houses became a school, later becoming a shop and eventually the Britannia Inn as it stands today.

Benjamin Huntsman's connections with the inn are of great interest. He was of Dutch origin and a clockmaker in Doncaster before he came to live in Handsworth in 1740. He was not satisfied with the imported Swedish and German materials he had to use for clock springs and pendulums and this led to his experiments with steel. He found he could purify ordinary steel by melting it to a high temperature in sealed clay crucibles with a flux, the composition of which he kept secret.

Owing to the increased demand for his steel Benjamin Huntsman then built new works in Church Street, Attercliffe. The story goes that Huntsman's foreman allowed a ragged tramp to sleep in a corner of the works, but the tramp was in fact a spy for a rival firm who saw enough of the new steel process to enable it to be copied.

Huntsman died in 1776, and as previously mentioned, was buried in Hill Top Cemetery, near the old Chapel. Over the years his grave fell into a sad state of neglect, but recently it has been cleaned and restored by the City Council. The inscription on the tombstone reads: Benjamin Huntsman of Attercliffe, Steel Refiner, Died June 20th, 1776 aged 72 years.

Carbrook Hall

At the end of Attercliffe Common, standing slightly back from the main road, is the ancient Carbrook Hall.

Carbrook was the home of the Blunt family as long ago as 1176. The Hall was built in delightful surroundings, the clear waters of the Don on the left, with woodlands and rural features front and right. Open ground extended at the rear (the main road, still called Attercliffe Common, being our only reminder of this) and there were very few buildings in the neighbourhood. In the distance could be seen the beautiful wooded slopes of Wincobank Hill.

Carbrook Hall 1910

By courtesy of Sheffield City Libraries

In the reign of Elizabeth I a Richard Fenton resided here, but in 1623 we find the hall in the possession of Thomas Bright of Bradway, a descendant of John Bright of Whirlow Hall.

In 1637 the hall passed to Stephen Bright, who was Lord of the Manor of Ecclesall in 1638. It was Stephen who, with the help of his brother John, the Vicar of Sheffield, helped to build the small Hill Top Chapel.

When 23 years of age, John Bright, who was the son of Stephen, took over the estate. John Bright was on the side of Parliament during the Civil War, which extended from 1642 to 1649, and he was made a Colonel in 1643. He was appointed Governor of Sheffield Castle when it was surrendered by royalist Forces in 1644, and he retired from Army Service in 1650.

During the years 1649 to 1660, John was Governor of York and Hull, and he was also High Sheriff of the County of York from 1654 to 1655. Charles II then made him a baronet and he eventually died in September, 1688.

The Hall then passed to Katherine, the daughter of John Bright. This lady married Sir Henry Liddall and they had a son whom they named John. When John Liddall became heir to the estate, he assumed the name of Bright, so the Hall was once again the home of the Bright family.

Later the Hall passed by various marriages through the

Thompson and Whetham families until, in the late 18th century we find the building was owned by Lucy Sotheran. From her it came into the ownership of her brother, Admiral Frank Sotheran, a gentleman who lived from 1776 to 1861.

It was the Admiral who closed the Bright estate by putting it into the open market and in 1819 it was bought by Thomas Booth & Company, who in turn sold it to George Bradford, the largest farmer in the district. George Bradford, who lived from 1787 to 1861, owned practically the whole of Attercliffe Common and a quantity of land towards Tinsley.

In 1855 George Bradford must have left the Hall for we find the owners were then the River Dun (Don) Company and the tenants the Carbrook Land Society.

From that time onwards the historic hall deteriorated and became, according to the records, a 'common beer house'. Today it is the Carbrook Hall Hotel and the landlord serves drinks to his customers in the parlour where, during the Civil War, many vital conferences were held.

This parlour is now the showplace of the hotel, a fine room twenty two feet long by eighteen feet wide beautifully panelled in oak. The ceiling is very excellent moulded plaster work and the very unusual carving on the oak fireplace was probably executed by Leonard Gill. This design is described as Wisdom Trampling on Ignorance and shows the figure of a man with his foot on the distended stomach of a prostrate figure, probably a woman.

Originally attached to the present Carbrook Hall was a large half timbered building, but this was demolished between 1777 and 1819. The ancient part of the present hall was built about 1623 and the 'secret' door in the old parlour probably led into the half timbered section. Over the parlour is a similar panelled room of the same date, but not in a very good condition.

Woodhill House

Backing on to the old Grimesthorpe Road stands a Georgian house called Woodhill. Built in the 18th century, it was the home of Colonel Fenton, the chief of the Militia during the stormy uprisings in Sheffield.

From the front windows of Woodhill the Colonel could look down over the fields and watch his troops being drilled, where now stands works and factories of busy, industrial Sheffield.

The cottage that housed the Colonel's coachman still remains, but this, with the former stables and coach houses, are in a derelict condition.

Page Hall

Page Hall, which incidently was the first suburban residence to be erected in Sheffield by a purely commercial man, is situated at the south end of Cammell Road.

A pleasant stone house of two and a half storeys, it was built in 1773, in what was, at that time, surroundings of great beauty.

The banker, Thomas Broadbent of 'The Old Banker's House', Hartshead, commenced the building of this house for his own use, but was unable to occupy it owing to the failure of his banking business in 1782. This caused Broadbent to mortgage the hall to James Milnes of Wakefield. It was then purchased by Mr Greaves, a merchant of Sheffield, whose son, George Bustard Greaves, sold it in 1834 to James Dixon, the founder of an electro-plating works in Sheffield.

Later the house became the N.U.T. Benevolent Orphanage, eventually to be converted into the present day flats.

Norwood Hall

Norwood Hall was probably built between 1710 and 1713, for an entry in the Manor Court Rolls of 1710 states that Robert Sorsbie surrendered in the Manor Court a messuage called Norwood and nine acres to the use of William Taylor of Sheffield.

William Taylor died in 1719 and during the following year the house was sold by Taylor's executives to John Grammar. At that time the house was described as 'a newly built messuage'.

Norwood then passed through a number of hands until in 1769 we find the hall and lands leased by William Walton of Hathersage to the noted Samuel Glanville, of the Angel Hotel, Sheffield. However, in 1775 Glanville assigned the lease to James Wheat and the Wheat family's association with the hall continued until James Clifton Wheat offered the house and lands to the Sheffield Corporation for 'laying out as a Garden City'. This offer was refused by the Corporation.

Charles Edward Vickers, of the Manor House, Ecclesall, then bought Norwood Hall and it was he who sold the estate to local trustees in 1918 for the use of Bishop Burrows, the Bishop of Sheffield. It was during Dr. Burrow's occupation that the hall acquired the name of 'Bishopsholme'.

In 1940 negotiations again commenced with the Sheffield Corporation and shortly afterwards Norwood Hall and lands became their property.

After using the house for various purposes, Norwood was left

Norwood Hall 1972

empty and unattended, it then became a prey for vandals and commenced to fall into ruin. In 1969 the Sheffield City Council applied for 'Listed Building Consent' to demolish the hall.

A number of interested people, which included the author, then formed a 'Norwood Group' to fight this proposal and as a result of the protests made, a Public Enquiry was held on 24th and 25th February, 1970. On 15th May, 1970, the Minister of Housing and Local Government gave his decision that the hall must not be demolished.

Though many schemes were put forward for use of the hall, these were rejected by the City Council and on 19th and 20th December, 1972 a further Public Enquiry was held. Once again the Council were informed that they must not demolish the building.

More schemes for the use of the hall were put forward, only to be dismissed and further vandalism and destruction took place. Then on Saturday, 5th June, 1976, very early in the morning, bulldozers commenced to demolish the building. The City Council stated afterwards that this had been necessary on the grounds of 'public safety'.

Thus ended the life of Norwood Hall and Sheffield lost its only Queen Anne building

Cannon Hall Cottages

Formerly standing at the side of the busy Barnsley Road, near the gates of the old Firvale Hospital, were the picturesque Cannon Hall Cottages.

These pleasant buildings were originally the sleeping accommodation for the grooms of Cannon Hall, but later they served as part of the old Firvale Workhouse.

They were converted into cottages in 1839 and this date appeared above the doorway on the centre building. The date stone read 'E1839S' the initials standing for Edward Smith, who converted the dwellings. The cottages were probably of the late 17th or early 18th century and they can be seen on the Fairbanks map of 1795.

Pitsmoor Toll Bar

At the junction of Barnsley Road, Burngreave Road and Pitsmoor Road stands the building that was formerly the Pitsmoor Toll Bar.

Pitsmoor Toll Bar

This was built in 1836 to replace an earlier one of 1759. The large wooden gates swung across Burngreave Road and Pitsmoor Road and tolls were levied there until 1876.

One of the largest toll payers at Pitsmoor, was Mr Pass, who worked a colliery at the end of Coal Pit Lane, which ran along the border of Abbeyfield Park. Mr Pass shared with the stage coaches the privilege of paying his tolls monthly instead of each time his carts passed through the toll gates.

A number of wayfarers travelling up Barnsley Road found they could by-pass the Pitsmoor Toll Bar and so save money, by turning up Osgathorpe Road. So, to prevent this loss of earnings a catchbar (small toll bar) was erected on the Barnsley Road at this point. The small narrow cottage of the catchbar could be seen up to a few years ago on the right hand side of the road approaching Sheffield. It has now been demolished.

Catch Bar House, Barnsley Road 1972

Abbeyfield House

This large stone house, situated in Abbeyfield Park, almost opposite the Pitsmoor Toll Bar, was built by Mr. Pass, as his own residence, at the end of the 18th century.

After the death of Mr. Pass, the fine house was occupied for the greater part of the 19th century by the Wake family, passing to the Greenwood family in the early 20th century. It is now in the possession of the Sheffield Parks Department Staff Training Centre.

The charming sundial on the corner of the house was erected by Bernard Wake in 1883.

The Pass Houses

Formerly standing on a little lane, now called Pass Houses Road, were a group of cottages in which lived some of the miners who were employed at the Pass colliery.

The Pass Houses 1972

Erected very early in the 18th century, amidst open fields, it was a common occurrence for farm animals to put their heads in through the open kitchen windows in search of tit-bits. An old lady living in one of the cottages, before they were demolished, informed the author that when she came to live there in 1906, the rent was two shillings and ninepence a week, the only water supply was from a tap on the wall outside, and all the lighting was by paraffin lamps. As a child she remembered her mother watching the old people going past her home on their way to the Union Workhouse at Firvale. These destitute people, too old to work, had to go into the workhouse, and be parted, man from wife, as the only alternative to starvation. The same old lady recalled her mother kneeling in prayer, with tears running down her cheeks, asking the Lord to spare her from such a bitter fate.

Wadsley Hall

This beautiful old hall near the bottom of Far Lane, stands on very ancient foundations. In 1409 Sir Robert de Wadsley had a licence to hold divine service in a chapel which was situated at the rear of the hall.

However, in 1722, George Bamforth, the Lord of the Manor, rebuilt the hall and it is his building we see today.

The old house has been owned by many interesting families, including in 1547, an Arthur Griff, yeoman; in 1557, the Swyft family; and in 1590, George, the Sixth Earl of Shrewsbury. Following George, Gilbert, the Seventh Earl owned the house until his death in 1616, when by descent, it passed to the Norfolks.

In 1750 it is recorded that the hall was occupied by the Creswick family, and Thomas Creswick, R.A. the famous landscape painter, was born there.

John Fowler, a surveyor, owned the hall in 1822, and in 1884 Sir John Fowler, famous as the designer of the Forth Bridge, bought the freehold. From him the estate passed to Sir John Edward Fowler, who was killed in the First World War. In 1914 Sir John gave the use of the hall to Belgian refugees, entirely rent free. When the war ended the estate was broken up, but a niece of one of the Fowlers, a Mrs. Campbell, continued to live there.

Later owners of the hall were the Longden family, Miss Mary Longden, following the tradition of the illustrious owners before her, keeping the house and grounds in excellent condition.

One of Miss Longden's hobbies was collecting ancient stone sinks and troughs to use as garden ornaments, but most of these

Wadsley Hall

have now been sold. However, in the grounds, is a stone cross, which was formerly part of the old Parish Church.

The present owners of the hall are Dr. and Mrs. W. Purcell, who took up residency there on 8th January, 1976.

The front door of Wadsley Hall has a half wooden door on the interior, which can be closed to cover up the upper glass panes. This was probably used as a protection against thieves.

The hall is stone built and the coat of arms of the Bamforths is carved on the date stone over the front doorway. The chapel that existed at the rear was removed about 156 years ago, having for a good many years before its demolition served as a cow house. However a number of outbuildings still exist, but most of these are the remains of Wadsley Hall Farm, the farm houses being situated just below the hall.

These farm houses are also kept in an excellent condition, and near the entrance to these is a 'pound', where stay horses and cattle were enclosed until claimed by the owners.

Travellers Inn

Standing back off Penistone Road North is the Travellers Inn, a building little altered on the exterior since it was erected in the 17th century. In what was formerly the kitchen is a large stone fireplace on which is carved the initials G.C. and the date 1697.

Formerly horse troughs stood in front of the inn, but these were removed about 26 years ago. In recent years the widening of Penistone Road has meant that the large courtyard that occupied the whole front has been removed, unfortunately destroying the ancient look of this former coaching inn.

Niagara House

Not very far from the Travellers Inn there stood Niagara House, an old building of uncertain date. It was stone built, had 15 rooms and near the back door had a stone mounting block.

Over seventy years ago the house belonged to a Mr. Clark, who held horse races on the Niagara Track which adjoined the house. It is believed that Mr. Clark eventually mortgaged the house to the Duke of Norfolk and later the Duke put in, as tenant, an employee named Staniforth. The Staniforth family resided at the house until 1957.

Burrowlee House

Burrowlee Road, off Penistone Road, is a Georgian house of great charm, though surrounded as it is by nineteenth century houses, it can easily be missed by the casual passer-by.

Burrowlee House was probably built upon the foundations of a much earlier building, as we know there was a dwelling house there as early as the sixteenth century.

In deeds of 1539 and 1557, the Creswick family were acquiring land in Burrowlee, and in a pre-nuptial agreement drawn up between Thomas Creswick and Henry Shawe in 1621, concerning the marriage of their respective son and daughter, William Creswick and Anne Shawe, specific mention is made of a house in this area.

An inquisition held after the death of Thomas Creswick in 1640 indicates that the Burrowlee property itself was worth only twelve shillings per annum, quite a modest sum even in those days, and the house was only a cottage. However Thomas possessed various other properties. All through the century the Creswicks referred to themselves as 'yeomen' and never 'gentlemen'.

The last Thomas Creswick died in 1686, leaving two daughters. The youngest one, Elizabeth, married Thomas Steade in 1696 and eventually the whole Burrowlee property came to her. The Steades were gentlemen and a prosperous family and it was Thomas and Elizabeth who built the present Burrowlee House in 1711. The date stone over the front doorway gives this date, with the initials 'T.S.'. In the will of Thomas Steade of 1738–9 he specifically mentions Burrowlee House, which he left to Elizabeth for her use for life.

Eventually one of their descendants, another Thomas Steade, married Melisande Pegge and the marriage settlement of 1776 settled on the bride the property of Burrowlee House.

Later the Steades acquired considerable other property and moved to Hillsborough Hall, renting Burrowlee to tenants of no particular note.

This fine old house now belongs to the Sheffield City Council who have restored the building to its previous magnificence. It is occupied as a Boys' Club, run by the South Yorkshire and Hallamshire Boys Clubs.

Burrowlee House has a very beautiful frontage, has a hipped roof and a stone balustrade over the three middle bays.

Old Corn Mill Water Wheel

A very interesting old water wheel is to be found at the bottom of

Stannington Road at Malin Bridge. This is one of the few undershoot wheels in the county, the water passing under the wheel instead of over the top as in most cases.

It is recorded that a Mr Parkin worked this grinding wheel in 1794, but in 1864 the wheel was in the hands of Butler, Wilson and Company.

In the great Sheffield Flood the superstructure was severely damaged and most of it washed away, but it was eventually repaired and continued as a grinding wheel. Later German Wilson changed the wheel into a machine shop, subsequently altered by his son into a corn mill.

When the mill was acquired by Mr D. Marsden, he found the wheel damaged and neglected, lying in the river. At his own expense he had workmen repair the wheel and it was set back on its original bearings. Although the machinery formally turned by the wheel still exists, the wheel is not now connected, but allowed to turn continually for the benefit of passing pedestrians.

After Mr. D. Marsden vacated the premises, they fell into a bad state of repair. However the Corn Mill is now the property of the Comet Discount Warehouse and this firm have renovated the buildings once again.

Langsett Road Toll Bar

On Langsett Road, Hillsborough, usually unnoticed by the people passing by, we find another of the old Sheffield toll bars, built in the early 19th century.

On the wall facing the main road can still be seen the jointing, where the gable of the gatehouse was connected to the present building.

This toll bar ceased to exist as such in 1875 and the gatehouse was demolished later when the road was widened.

Barber Nook House

Situated just off Barber Road and practically hidden by a large store, is a charming cottage called Barber Nook House.

Built around the year 1728, the cottage had for many years a workhouse as its neighbour. Barber Nook House was owned for many years by members of the Barber family, from whom Barber Road takes its name.

The present owner of the cottage is Mr. K. Ramsell, who, though carrying out much modernisation, has retained a great deal of its old world atmosphere.

Barber Nook House

Broom Hall

The earlier portion of Broom Hall was built in the time of Henry VIII, that is from 1509 to 1547. The estate first belonged to the De Ecclesalls and extended from Crookesmoor to Sheffield Castle. Later the estate was settled by Robert de Ecclesall on Joan de Wanton and this passed to the Wickersley family through marriage.

The Wickersleys were a very ancient family, one of them being the co-founder with Richard de Busli, of Roche Abbey. The last of the Wickersleys, Nicholas, died in 1528, leaving a daughter who married Robert Swyft and by this marriage Robert acquired Wickersley, Broom Hall and other estates. Robert Swyft was first mentioned in 1532 when he made Broom Hall his principal residence. Robert was also principal agent for Sheffield Castle and one of the Twelve Capitol Burgesses of Sheffield.

Robert's offspring were all daughters, the youngest Anne, marrying Richard Jessop, son of William Jessop of Rotherham.

Broom Hall

On the partition of the estates of Robert Swyft, Broom Hall had passed to Richard Jessop, along with North Lees Hall in Derbyshire. There were seven generations of the Jessop family at Broom Hall and the last one, William, died in 1734, leaving only daughters. The estate was then held by his daughters and co-heirs. Two of these died unmarried and the Rev. James Wilkinson, the last surviving son of the elder of the two married daughters, inherited Broom Hall.

James Wilkinson became one of Sheffield's most notable citizens. He was Vicar of Sheffield from 1754 until his death in 1805 and he was also the local magistrate. It was during his ownership of Broom Hall that the fine East Wing was built.

In 1791 a riotous mob attempted to burn Broom Hall, but little damage was done except for parts of the library and some books were destroyed.

After the death of Vicar Wilkinson, the property passed to one of his relations, Philip Gell of Hopton, who resold it in 1826 to John Watson of Shirecliffe Hall. Broom Hall was then divided into three dwellings and let to a series of tenants. Various private schools occupied part of the premises in the early 19th century, whilst another part was used as a farmhouse until the middle of the century, when one hundred and four acres of land associated with the Hall were laid out as a superior housing estate.

The Hall was occupied up to the Second World War by a firm of solicitors, then except for the Georgian East Wing, was largely unoccupied.

On the 4th August, 1970, the then owners, the United Society for the Propagation of the Gospel, applied to the Sheffield City Council for permission to completely demolish the Tudor portion of the building and to erect a six storey office block. This application was rightly refused.

In 1971 Broom Hall was acquired by the Stag Industrial Holdings Ltd., who in May, 1972, made application to erect a two storey office block within the grounds on the east side. They then wished to restore Broom Hall and to convert it into high class offices. Permission was refused by the City Council on the grounds that the site was within a Conservation Area and that the erection of offices on the site would be detrimental to the area.

An appeal was then made to the Secretary of State by Stag Holdings Ltd. against the Corporation decision and a Public Enquiry was held on 20th June, 1972. On 2nd October, 1972, the Secretary of State gave notice that he had dismissed the appeal on the grounds that the benefits of the preservation of the Hall would be overuled by the disadvantages of the commercial use of the grounds.

In 1973 the Hall was bought by the internationally known designer, Mr. David Mellor, who lived in Park Lane, only a few yards away from the site of the now ruinous house. The first stage of the restoration was to the Georgian East Wing and this was converted into a studio workshop for which Mr. Mellor won a European Architectural Heritage Year award. Work was then begun on the rest of the Hall and the ancient timber portion of the 16th century, was completely restored. This is now the living accommodation for Mr. Mellor and his family. A ruined portion of the hall built in Victorian times has been removed and the grounds landscaped.

Thanks to Mr. David Mellor the Hall has regained its former beauty, and is now an historic building of which Sheffield can be proud.

Stag Inn

Before the year 1800 there was a decayed old alehouse situated across the top of what is now Cemetery Road. This old inn was owned by the Rev. Alexander Mackenzie who, being a good business man, had it pulled down and a new inn, which he called the 'Stag's Head', built on Psalter Lane to replace it. This was in a perfect position on the old turnpike road, for the coaches, after the long pull up Sharrow Lane, were always ready for a rest and refreshment.

The 'Stag's Head', a name derived from the crest of the Mackenzie family, was first let to a publican in the year 1805, and has now given over 173 years of service.

It has been proposed that sometime in the future the 'Stag' will be pulled down and a large new hotel built on the site of the present premises.

Sharrow Green Cottage

Situated at the top of Sharrow Vale Road, at its junction with Psalter Lane, is 'Sharrow Green Cottage', a pleasant house built in 1795 by the aforementioned Rev. Alexander Mackenzie. From this reverend gentleman the cottage passed by descent to Captain Toll who sold it to John Smith in 1851. In 1862, John Smith, in turn, sold the property to Henry Wilson, owner of the very old snuff mills nearby.

In 1966 the cottage came under the ownership of Mr. J. Granville Barber, who beautifully restored the interior, meanwhile retaining the old world charm of this delightful building.

Sharrow Green Cottage

Bellwood Photography Ltd.

Today Sharrow Green Cottage is the residence of Mr. and Mrs. Graham Cohen, who acquired the property in 1970. Both the exterior and interior are kept in beautiful condition, the rooms being furnished with period pieces to give added character.

Roadside Cottage

On Cherrytree Road, just off Psalter Lane, we see the remains of the little medieval hamlet of Cherrytree. Unfortunately only two of the old cottages now remain, even though the preservationists put up a long fight to try and save the other cottages which were in excellent condition.

One of the cottages still standing today is Roadside Cottage, or 'Cherrytree House', as it was formerly called.

This charming residence was built in 1635 by Thomas Ludlam, who occupied the cottage for a good many years. It is recorded that in 1780 the owner was then one Mary Naw, but in 1828 we find it converted into the Bowling Green Inn.

It appears a Thomas Jenkinson, a hammer manufacturer and publican, kept the inn from that time and the gardens at the rear were known as Cherrytree Hill Bowling Green and Tea Gardens.

It is said that beneath these gardens there existed an underground ballroom, the dancing being illuminated by many Chinese lanterns.

Thomas Jenkinson died in October, 1841, and after some years the building fell into a state of neglect. After passing through a number of hands, the property was bought in 1946 by a Mr. Stewardson, who made a number of alterations and restorations, making the cottage the pleasant building we see today.

The present owners of Roadside Cottage are Mr. and Mrs. L. H. Tattersall, who have made a certain number of alterations and improvements to the old building. However these in no way interfere with the pleasant period atmosphere of the house.

Wistaria Cottage

Situated at the lower end of Cherrytree Road is Wistaria Cottage, a house built in 1765 by Robert Bagshaw. A stone over the front doorway gives this date, together with the initials 'R.B.R.' Robert Bagshaw, a scythesmith by trade, and his wife, lived at the cottage until 1783, when it passed into the hands of George Bagshaw, of Woodend in Beauchief, and his descendants.

Wistaria Cottage

Bellwood Photography Ltd.

In 1852 the deeds of the house show the owner was then David Smith of Sheffield, who lived there until 1858. From 1859, Henry Newbould of Sharrow and his heirs occupied the house, but in 1909 it was acquired by Albert Rhodes of Dronfield. In 1926, Mr Rhodes' daughter, Mrs Mary Haigh, became the owner and she still occupies the cottage at the present time.

Wistaria Cottage is in excellent condition, only a few structural alterations having been made to the interior. The original oak beams still support the ceilings and there is a low vaulted cellar under the house. The exterior of the cottage has been stuccoed to resurface the immensely thick stone walls.

Hunter's Bar

On the traffic island at the bottom of Brocco Bank, forming a centre piece in the middle of the busy Ecclesall Road, stand the gate posts of what was once Hunter's Toll Bar. The use of the toll bar came to an end at midnight on 31st October, 1884. Crowds of people had assembled at the bar as it reached midnight and the last person to pass through was Mr. Haigh, a cab and coach proprietor, of Glossop Road. At 12 o'clock, to cheers from the crowd, John Speer, the toll collector, his occupation gone, simply locked the doors of his toll house and walked away. The crowd then lifted the gate off its hinges and threw it over a wall into a nearby field.

When the toll bar house was demolished to widen the road, the stone gate posts were used for the entrance to Endcliffe Park nearby, but later when the traffic island was made the posts were replaced in the exact position they had occupied for so long. The gate or bar that is now fitted to the posts is quite modern.

Near the bar, the Georgian house in which Hunter lived can still be seen as part of the Hunter House Hotel. When built, as a farm house, around the year 1700, the building would occupy a fine position overlooking the countryside which is now Endcliffe Park. Now the old house has for its neighbours villas of the 19th century and can easily be missed by people travelling on Ecclesall Road.

Endcliffe Hall

The original name of Endcliffe was 'Elcliffe' and the estate on which the first Hall was built can be traced back to 1333 when a grant was made to John de Elcliffe. The estate then extended to the far side of Brincliffe and reached down to Heeley. Other family

Hunter's Bar

names in connection which the property are John de Cliff and Henry de Tapton of the 14th century. The estate is again mentioned in a deed by Robert Burrus of Elcliffe in 1577.

The first Endcliffe Hall was probably erected in the reign of George II, but it is possible that there was an even earlier building on the site.

William Hodgson acquired the property in 1818 from the Broom Hall Estate and this included 50 acres of land, plus two houses, and cost him £6,700. William Hodgson is described as a merchant and the Hodgsons were a well known Sheffield family in the 19th century. Later Henry Wilkinson, a silversmith, purchased the property from Hodgson and he lived at Endcliffe Hall for some years. Eventually he moved to Endcliffe Edge, close by.

In August, 1860, John Brown bought the Hall and 40 acres of land from Wilkinson.

John Brown was born in Favell's Yard, Fargate, in 1816. He became famous in the steel trade, was a Master Cutler and received a knighthood in 1867.

Immediately John Brown acquired Endcliffe Hall he pulled the old building down and in its place he built the mansion we see today. It is built in the Italionate style and was constructed mostly by Sheffield workmen. It had a grand salon and other fine rooms, which were mostly used, during John Brown's occupation, for the exhibition of works of art and statuary. In the centre of the house is a very fine grand staircase.

Sir John Brown sold the house in 1895, a year before his death, for £26,000 to Barber Brothers and Wortley for building land. Thankfully however, it was never used for that purpose.

In 1916 Endcliffe Hall was bought on behalf of the Territorial Association for the Hallamshire Battalion, the York and Lancaster Regiment, and except for a period during the First World War when it was used as a Military Hospital, it remained the Hallamshire's Headquarters until the battalion was disbanded in 1968.

Still in Military hands, this fine old house is now used by 'D' Company, 1st Battalion Yorkshire Volunteers.

Stumperlowe Hall

In the pleasant district of Fulwood, situated at the corner of Slayleigh Lane and Stumperlowe Hall Road, is Stumperlowe Hall, a building considerably altered and rebuilt in 1854.

The Hall has had many important occupants, including the Mitchell family and it is recorded that as far back as 1397, this

Endcliffe Hall

Stumperlowe Hall

Bellwood Photography Ltd.

family owned the lands and property of Stumperlowe.

Thomas Mitchell was one of the first of the Twelve Capital Burgesses appointed by the Charter of Philip and Mary in 1554, and his son, Robert was one of the first governors of the old Sheffield Grammar School, named in the Charter of King James the First.

However, Robert Mitchell had no sons and when he died Stumperlowe Hall came into the possession of his daughter, Margaret, who married Henry Hall, of Midhope. Their son Robert, is believed to have been the builder of the present hall, about the year 1650.

In 1716, at the Manor Court of Sheffield, the Hall family surrendered Stumperlowe Hall to Daniel Gascoigne of Sheffield and John Hawksworth, a lead merchant. The latter gentleman occupied the house for the greater part of the 18th century, until it came into the possession of the Glossop family of Shirecliffe Hall.

From 1802 the property passed through the hands of Christopher Oates of High House, Sheffield; John Woodcroft of Bennett Grange, Fulwood; John Armitage of Ilkley; eventually in 1854 becoming the residence of Henry Isaac Dixon.

It was Henry Dixon who considerably rebuilt Stumperlowe Hall, giving the building the exterior we see today.

Lady Kenning, well known in connection with the motorcar firm, lived at the hall from 1957 until her death in 1974.

The present owners of this beautiful old house are Mr. and Mrs. Reginald V. Cam, who, during some interior alterations, discovered part of an old kitchen that had obviously been hidden by the rebuilding in the 19th century.

Slayleigh Cottages

These old cottages, situated near Chorley Drive, were first mentioned in 1637, in a survey made by Harrison for the Lord of the Manor, the Earl of Surrey. The fields on which the cottages stand belonged to Thomas Machin, a large land holder, well known at that time in Hallam. The stone used for the building came from a field in front of the cottages, which was known as 'Stone Field'.

In 1772 it is recorded that the owner was John Burton of Bramley Hall, Handsworth and the tenant was Joseph Lockwood.

At that time and up to the middle nineteenth century, the cottages were surrounded by fields, Chorley Road being simply a cart track known to the inhabitants of Fulwood as 'Back Lane'.

The two cottages, which are the residence of Mr and Mrs C.J. Thornton, are now converted into one, and with the adjoining dove cote, they make a pleasant oasis amidst the modern houses of the district.

Fulwood Chapel

Fulwood Chapel was built in 1729, under the provision of a will of William Ronksley of Gunthwaite, for the inhabitants of Fulwood, who were dissenters from the doctrines of the Church of England. It was endowed by Mr. Ronksley with four hundred pounds. The first minister of the Chapel was the Rev. Jeremiah Gill, who occupied the pastorate from 1729 to 1758.

The £400 invested for the Chapel seems to have had a sporadic existence, for in 1854 the Rev. Hugh Rhodes, the minister at that time, informed the Commissioners that he had received no interest or 'any part thereof' for the benefit of the Chapel. Though not expressly given by the terms of the will to the trustees of the Chapel, it is quite probable that it was received by them, for Mr. Rhodes had reason to believe that it was entered in the books of Messrs. Shores' Bank, at Sheffield. It appears that a member of the firm had at different times always been one of the trustees of Fulwood Chapel.

However, we find that in 1779, the principal sum of £400 was in

Fulwood Stocks

the hands of Benjamin Roebuck and Sons, Bankers of Sheffield, and the interest was paid by them until their failure, when the money was handed to a relative, Francis Fenton. He was a member of the firm of Roebuck and Fenton, also bankers, who paid interest to the minister until 1808, when that bank also failed and the £400 was lost.

In 1863 Mr. Rhodes informed the Commissioners that new trustees of the Chapel had been appointed, but when Mr. Rhodes died in 1873, the Chapel shut its doors and remained closed until the summer of 1896.

Later that same year, the surviving trustee, Michael Hunter, appointed new trustees, all Unitarians, and the Chapel was re-opened for services on Sunday afternoons.

A burial ground formerly existed in front of Fulwood Chapel and a number of graves were discovered when Whiteley Lane was widened. Nearby was a mineral spring, known in the 18th century as Fulwood Spa, and used by the local inhabitants to cure many ills.

In the garden near the doorway of the Chapel are the stocks which formerly stood on the village green or common land. For many years the stone pillars were used as gateposts at a house in Whiteley Lane, but now, complete with wooden stocks and padlock, they stand at the front of the old Chapel as a reminder of the punishments of bygone years.

Fulwood Hall

This beautiful old hall, situated in Harrison Lane, stands at a height of 870 feet, on the northern side of the Mayfield Valley.

Built in the shape of a letter L, of local stone, it has a date stone of 1620, but this is probably only the date of some alterations, for Fulwood Hall is mentioned in deeds of the time of Henry VII. The owners at that time were the Fox family and the hall continued in their hands until George surrendered the estate in 1707.

It appears that this gentleman, together with Henry Bright of Whirlow Hall and a number of others, lived a life of such gaiety and indulgence that all their money wasted away, their estates having eventually to be sold.

Later Fulwood Hall passed, by purchase, to the Greaves family, who resided there for many years. The hall then passed through a considerable number of hands, until in 1942, it became the property of the well known Fairest family.

The late Mr. Morgan Fairest, during the course of restoration, made an interesting discovery, when behind two comparatively modern fireplaces, he found ancient stone chimney pieces.

Whirlow Hall

If we walk along Broad Elms Lane, at Ecclesall, we find a narrow lane that is a very good example of the original boundary roads, very little changed since the time it was first made. This leads to Whirlow Lane, where we find Whirlow Hall Farm, once the home of the famous Bright family, who settled at Whirlow in the 15th century.

When John Bright died in 1586, he left three sons, Henry who succeeded to the family estates at Whirlow; Thomas of Carbrook Hall; and John of Banner Cross Hall. Successive heirs of the Brights remained at Whirlow until about 1718, when Henry Bright parted with the estates to Sir John Statham of Tideswell. The sale of the Whirlow estates was caused by Henry Bright squandering his money in gambling and other forms of low living and this type of life eventually brought him to an early grave.

Bellwood Photography Ltd.

Fulwood Hall

In 1726, Sir John Statham resold the estates to Thomas Hollis, who was a Sheffield cutler. In deeds dated the 17th and 18th May, 1726, Thomas Hollis conveyed the Whirlow estates to Trustees for the further endowment of the Hollis Hospital in Sheffield. This was for the benefit of widows of cutlers and other persons employed in the particular manufactures of Sheffield.

Whirlow Hall was then converted into tenements and remained in existence until the year 1795, when the eastern portion was taken down, to be followed in 1842 by total demolition.

The present house, which is now owned by Mr. H.B. Ellis, was probably built with many of the stones from the original building.

However, most of the farm buildings are original and there is a very interesting cruck building which probably dates from the 14th century.

There also remains an hayloft door, made of solid oak, with a carved date of 1652. This ancient door has no hinges, but is fastened to a pole that swivels in stone slots. There was formerly another wooden door of this type, likewise dated 1652, but this was lost when the old cowhouse was demolished.

Abbeydale Industrial Hamlet

A very unique number of buildings can be seen on Abbeydale Road South near Beauchief Gardens. These are the Abbeydale Works, an 18th century industrial hamlet and scythe works.

At this museum of one of Sheffield's oldest industries, it is possible to trace the manufacture of steel edge tools from the raw materials to the finished product.

Also preserved at these works in an early furnace for producing crucible steel of the type invented by Benjamin Huntsman in 1742. The crucibles in which the steel was made were produced here and it is still possible to see the workshop where the clay was kneaded before being made into 'pots', as the crucibles were commonly called.

The steel, which was of a very high quality, was made from iron and scrap, together with a carbon flux, which was heated in the 'pot' for about four hours.

After the crucible was taken from the furnace, the slag was skimmed off and the molten metal poured into moulds. It was then allowed to cool to a red heat before being removed. When cold the ingot was then tested and if found satisfactory it was roughly forged into shape. This was done by reheating in a hearth in the tilt forge, after which waterdriven tilt hammers were used.

These hammers were lifted by cogs on a main shaft which tilted

Abbeydale Industrial Hamlet

Courtesy of
Sheffield City Museums

them to give the forging action needed to sandwich a piece of carbon steel between pieces of wrought iron. This gave great strength to the cutting edge of the tool.

The grinding machinery was driven by an 18 foot water wheel and also an horizontal steam engine, which was added in the 19th century, for use during times of water shortage.

Near the grinding workshop was a hefting and boring shop, again driven by water power, and there was also a large warehouse, various offices and a row of workmen's cottages.

The Abbeydale Industrial Hamlet was restored by the Council for the Conservation of Sheffield Antiquities, who raised almost fifty-two thousand pounds for the work. It was handed over to the Sheffield City Council in 1970 and it is now administered by the City Museums. The hamlet is open to the public seven days a week and special working days are arranged throughout the year when demonstrations of the old crafts are given.

Beauchief Abbey

The remains of Beauchief Abbey are situated just off Abbey Lane, admist very pleasant surroundings.

The Abbey was founded by Robert Fitz Ranulf, Lord of Alfreton, about 1183. It was dedicated to Archbishop Beckett and the Virgin Mary and was given to the White Canons of the Premonstratention Order, some of whom originally came from Welbeck to settle at Beauchief.

Though the Abbey was comparatively small, it was a wealthy house, having a large estate which extended as far as Greenhill. Also the abbey possessed lands or estates at Woodseats, Ecclesall, Fulwood, Chesterfield, Eckington, Staveley, Dronfield, Dore and Totley.

The establishment of Beauchief was an Abbot, twenty-three canons, eight chantry priests and a number of lay brethren.

The Abbey buildings followed the normal pattern of such houses, but the church had rather a long nave considering that there is no evidence that it was ever used as a parish church. The church, which ran east to west, was over-all 200 feet long by 26 feet wide, and had transepts, but no aisles. The refectory was on the south side of the cloister, with the chapter house on the east side.

On the whole, the Abbey seems to have been run efficiently, but there were occasional lapses. For instance, when Beauchief was visited on 20th October, 1472, it was found 'That the keys of the church and the cloister are not kept in proper places, nor are the church and cloister locked up at proper hours. Also, that in the

Beauchief Abbey

evening, after complines, the brethren go outside the cloister, stay up so long, and get so much to drink that at midnight, when matins should be said, they cannot keep awake. Also, that the brethren go outside the monastery, not together as according to the statutes, they should, but one goes one way and another goes another way, every man as he pleases.'

In a visit made on 25th May, 1488, the report mentions that the Abbey had 24 oxen, 28 sheep and 12 pigs. It also stated that in the monastery they consumed each week, 10 bushels of wheat, 16 bushels of oats and 4 bushels of barley.

In 1490 the Abbey engaged a teacher to instruct such 'boys and novices as the convent shall name' in grammar and singing. Visitors sent by Henry VIII found no fault with the running of the monastery.

The Abbey continued to function until the Dissolution on the 4th February, 1537, when the Abbot, John Sheffield, and twelve canons surrendered it to the King. At the time of the suppression the revenues of the house were valued at £126: 3s: 4d. and the site, with the park, and 260 acres, were granted to Sir Nicholas Strelley for £223. Sir Nicholas also received the grange at Strawberry Lee, Totley.

The rest of the Abbey estates and lands went to various people, including Francis Talbot, the Earl of Shrewsbury; Sir Francis Leake; the Cavendish family; the Duke of Portland; the Fanshaws; and Sir William West.

The Strelley family were at that time Lords of the Manor of Ecclesall, but in 1648 the Beauchief estates passed to the family of Pegge, through the marriage of Gertrude Strelley, the sole heiress, with Edward, son of Edward Pegge, of Ashbourne, Derbyshire.

It was Edward Pegge who, about the year 1662, built the little church we see today. This church was added on to the still standing tower of the Abbey.

It is then recorded 'In 1662, Nathaniel Baxter, who had been a minister, being in these parts, fell into company with Edward Pegge, Esq. of Beauchief Hall, a very sober gentleman, who invited him to give a sermon in an old Abbey Church, called Beauchief, and he complied with the motion; after this, he agreed to let his steward give him sixteen pounds a year to do service therein; so Master Baxter sought a wife, bought a little estate in Woodseats Dale, hard by, and lived there many years.'

As previously mentioned, the tower of the Abbey is original, but unfortunately it lost its top storey and large west window. This window has now been restored, but not to the original tracery design. Of the church, the west wall, the woodwork and roof are all of the date 1662. The pews are of the box type, arranged to provide separate seating accommodation for the lord of the manor, his servants, estate agent and farm servants.

The finials of the pews display the arms of Strelley and Pegge, in three arrangements. There is also an interesting hymn board of the late 18th century, with the arms of the Pegge-Burnells on the rear.

Two arched doorways, one Norman and the other 13th century, have been at some time moved from their original positions and are now sited at either side of the exterior of the Abbey tower.

During excavations in 1925, two stone coffins were found containing human bones. It is most likely that these were abbots, though it is impossible to identify them now. Examination of the remains showed that one of the men was young and tall, whilst the other was old and short in stature.

The wooded hill to which the Normans gave the name Beauchief, or 'Beautiful Head', still stands above the ruins and as most of the land adjacent is in use as golf courses, the Abbey still occupies a delightful and charming situation.

Beauchief Hall

Beauchief Hall

In the year 1573 the Beauchief estates were granted to Sir Nicholas Strelley, but passed to the family of Pegge through the marriage of Gertrude Strelley, the sole heiress, with Edward, son of Edward Pegge, of Ashbourne, in 1648.

It was Edward Pegge, High Sheriff of Derbyshire in 1664, who built the handsome Beauchief Hall in 1671.

The hall stands a short distance away from Beauchief Abbey and was built largely from stones taken from this ancient pile.

Edward Pegge died in 1679, aged 58, and was buried in the Abbey. The estates then passed through the hands of Christopher Pegge, Strelley Pegge and Peter Pegge, the last named gentleman assuming the name of Burnell in 1784, on being declared one of the heirs of D'Arcy Burnell, of Winkburn in Nottinghamshire.

When he died in 1836, without issue, Peter Pegge-Burnell left his estate to his nephew, Broughton Benjamin Steade, who then assumed by royal licence, the surnames and arms of Pegge-Burnell.

The Pegge-Burnells owned Beauchief Hall until 1909, when it was rented to William Wilson, this gentleman eventually buying the hall in 1922. Later it became the home of A. Kingford Wilson, a former Master Cutler.

From that time the house has passed through a number of hands, which include being used as offices by a local furnishing company.

However, in 1958 the hall and grounds were acquired by the De La Salle College, the grounds being used as playing fields for the college boys. The hall was then leased to the Beauchief Independent Grammar School for Girls. It is now used by the De La Salle College Teachers and Staff Association.

Since Beauchief Hall has been owned by the College, a certain amount of restoration has been accomplished and the oak panelling in a number of rooms, which had at some time been painted, has now been stripped and cleaned and the panelling brought back to its former appearance.

Most of the beauty of Beauchief Hall is in the architecture of the exterior. However in the hall is a fine alabaster fireplace, with a simpler fireplace of the same material in the dining room. The corridors have red floor tiles, a number of them showing the arms of the Pegge-Burnells.

Jordanthorpe Hall

Situated near the large traffic roundabout, at the corner of Norton Lane and Cinderhill Lane is Jordanthorpe Hall.

For many years the hall was the home of the Linley family and the Linleys of Jordanthorpe appear to have been connected with the celebrated Elizabeth Linley, who became the wife of Sheridan. It was she who was painted by the famous artist Gainsborough, as 'The Maid of Bath'.

At the hall, Linley Sambourne, an artist, spent his childhood, little realizing that before his death in 1910, he would leave quiet Jordanthorpe for the hustle and bustle of Fleet Street in London, to be entrusted with the drawing of the chief cartoons for the magazine 'Punch'.

Originally Jordanthorpe Hall stood in a large paddock, but the largest part of this was removed when the traffic island was constructed.

For many years the hall was used as flats, but now it has been completely restored and is used as the staff quarters of the Mossbrook Residential School for Physically Handicapped Children, which is situated nearby.

Chantrey's Cottage

Further on Cinderhill Lane, adjacent to the Mossbrook School, is the cottage in which the famous sculptor, Sir Francis Chantrey, was born.

Chantrey was born on 7th April, 1781, and for part of his childhood he was employed as a 'Milk boy', work that meant rising very early in the morning and with large cans of milk slung on the sides of his donkey, making his way down the country lanes to Sheffield market.

Later Chantrey was put to work by his mother in a grocer's shop in Sheffield, but this was not to his liking and he shortly afterwards changed his employment to another shop nearby in High Street, which specialized in oil paintings and engravings.

After his apprenticeship Chantrey had a studio for a time at 24 Paradise Square, where he would paint portraits of the gentry of Sheffield for a few guineas. Among the portraits he painted were those of his old schoolmaster, Thomas Fox; his old friend Nicholas Jackson and two vicars of Sheffield, the Rev. James Wilkinson and the Rev. Thomas Sutton. One of Chantrey's friends was the poet and hymn writer, James Montgomery, and he made many portrait sketches of him.

Chantrey's Cottage *Bellwood Photography Ltd.*

Later Chantrey left Sheffield for London, there working as a woodcarver's assistant for five shillings per day, but he found this a very miserable existence.

However Chantrey met and became friends with Benjamin West, the President of the Royal Academy at that time and from then on Chantrey went from strength to strength. He modelled and painted portraits and in 1807 he wrote in a letter that he was working on eight portraits in his room, some nearly finished, at twenty guineas each. He also attended the Academy classes every evening from 6 to 8 o'clock.

In 1814 Chantrey made a bust of Samuel Shore of Meersbrook and one of Dr. John Browne, which was placed in the Royal Infirmary. When the Cutlers' Hall was built in 1832, he gave to this building casts of his busts of James Watt, Sir Walter Scott, George Canning and John Playfair.

Among the many statues that Chantrey executed were King George III, in the Guildhall, London; Sir Stanford Raffles, Sir John Malcolm, James Watt, Francis Horner and Sir Walter Scott, all in Westminster Abbey. In St Paul's Cathedral are busts of General Rolls Gilespie and Bishop Heber, the latter being the composer of the hymn 'From Greenland's Icy Mountains'. In the Natural History Museum is the statue of Sir Joseph Banks and a bust of this great naturalist and traveller is at Burlington House.

There are many other works by Chantrey in London, Liverpool, Manchester, Canterbury, Lichfield (the famous 'Sleeping Children'), Norwich, Rochester, Durham, Exeter, Salisbury etc.

Sir Francis made statues of three Kings and one of Queen Victoria, and he found great favour with all these royal personages.

In August, 1840, Chantrey paid his last visit to Norton and in 1910 Herbert Rhodes, the ninety year old postmaster at Old Norton Post Office, said he remembered, as a boy, seeing Chantrey upon his last visit to his birthplace.

When Chantrey died in November, 1841, his body was brought from London back to Norton, the journey taking six days. The hearse and mourning coach were each drawn by four horses and were preceded by four people on horseback.

On the Monday when they arrived at Norton, the cortege went to the Oakes for breakfast, given by W.J. Bagshawe. At the churchyard ceremony were many of Chantrey's friends and all the children from his old school.

Chantrey's grave lies on the south side of the Church of St. James and the vault is covered by a huge slab of Granite, with the inscription cut very deeply. In the same tomb lie Chantrey's mother, father and grandfather.

Hazelbarrow Farm

Not very far from Chantrey's cottage is Hazelbarrow Farm, a place of great interest to the local historian. The present farmhouse is built upon the site of the ancient Hazelbarrow Hall, which was built by the Frechevilles in the 16th century.

Even before this a number of buildings must have occupied this site, for we know that William de Haselbyre lived here before 1290. From the 14th century Hazelbarrow belonged to the Selioke family and it continued in this family until 1580 when William Selioke sold the land to the Frechevilles.

In 1635 Lord Frecheville sold Hazelbarrow to the Morewoods of Alfreton for £2,450. One of the daughters of Anthony Morewood, who was Sheriff of the County in 1649, and who lived at Hazelbarrow; married Henry Goring of Lyden, Sussex, about 1670, and Hazelbarrow passed to the Gorings.

Sir Charles Goring sold the estate in 1671 to John Storie, a lead merchant, and Storie's sister Margaret, his heiress, married Ferdinande Wingfield, of Wakefield, in whose family the estate remained for many years.

The last inhabitant of Hazelbarrow Hall, who was also the owner, was Storie Wingfield, who died in 1729, leaving money for the poor boys of Norton to be sent to the 'Gramer Schole'.

In 1784 the property went to Wingfield Wildman, after which it had a number of tenants until it was demolished in the early 19th century.

Remains of Hazelbarrow Hall can still be seen, for part of the rear wall of the hall is now a retaining wall for the farmhouse garden. In the wall, two windows and a low doorway form an interesting feature and near the front of the house two ancient stone gateposts remain to remind us of this historic old hall.

Today Hazelbarrow is farmed by Mr. L. Elliott and the cottage is the residence of Mr. E.C. Waller.

Ruins of Hazelbarrow Hall

Old Norton Post Office

At the top of School Lane, near the entrance to Oakes Park, was once a group of picturesque cottages, one of them being the former Old Norton Post Office.

Built in the 17th century, it was closed as a Post Office on 31st October, 1939. The closing marked the retirement of Mrs. Selina Rhodes who, though nearly eighty years of age, had carried on all the postal business in the village after the death of her husband in 1910. The post office was run by various members of the Rhodes family for one hundred and seven years.

The post office, together with the other cottages and the gardens that surrounded them, made a favourite study for artists and they were sketched and painted many times over the years.

In September, 1973, the Post Office and other cottages were put up for sale, with planning consent to convert the cottages into fashionable homes.

After being sold, the gardens were stripped and the cottages, including the post office, were converted and enlarged for luxury living.

In 1974 the old post office was offered for sale for £27,000 and the remainder of the cottages for a total of £93,500!

Maugherhay

A hundred yards or so, on the opposite side of School Lane, is Maugherhay, formerly an inn, with a cluster of cottages round about.

Now only a few converted cottages remain, of what must have been a truly delightful spot.

The Inn was called 'The Bowling Green House' in the early 19th century and had a bowling green adjacent. Later when 'Norton Green', a large house in School Lane was built, a portion of the old Bowling Green House was incorporated in the new structure.

Norton Green was rebuilt and enlarged by Mr. Addy in 1866, and had in the grounds, for many years, a little school which Sir Francis Chantrey attended when a boy. Unfortunately the school, which bore a stone bearing the inscription 'This School Rebuilt and Enlarged in 1787', was demolished to make way for modern homes. The fine house called Norton Green was also demolished in 1973.

The origin of the name Maugherhay is a matter for conjecture, for formerly the name had always been pronounced 'Magathay'. Addy, one of Sheffield's historians, considered the name had derived from 'mageth', a maid, and 'hay', an enclosure, indicating a place where milkmaids drove their cows to be milked.

The Oakes

In the beautiful Oakes Park at Norton, stands 'The Oakes', the home of the noted Bagshawe family and a house of great historical worth and beauty.

The present house is obviously not the first to be built on this site, for The Oakes is first mentioned in deeds of 1590. At that time the owner was John Parker, to be followed by Gabriel Parker in 1616.

According to the Bagshawe Deeds and Papers, The Oakes, with all its outbuildings, was then nortgaged to a Robert Boulton of Offcote, for £355, to be repaid within a year. Obviously that mortgage was not paid within the time specified, for in 1642 we find that Robert Boulton was selling the house and estate to Henry Wigfall of Eckington for £450. In 1668 the property passed from the Wigfall family to John Lee of Hazelbarrow and Thomas Bagshawe of Tideswell.

However in 1672, Francis Barker of Lees Hall, bought the 'newly built messuage' for £1,600, so therefore, this date must be approximately the date of the present building.

The Oakes, Oakes Park

Gates to the Oakes

In April, 1673, Francis Barker sold the property to Jonathon Staniforth of Rotherham, and he in turn, sold it to Joseph Moorwood of Bradfield, in December, 1675.

A further deed shows the sale of The Oakes, Farm and 12 Closes, to Henry Gill of Hemsworth, for £1,240 and it is this last deed that brings the Bagshawe family into the ownership of The Oakes. This happened when Elizabeth Gill, eldest daughter of Henry, married Richard Bagshawe in 1699.

Since that time the house has passed through the hands of eleven members of the Bagshawe family, one of the most noted being Sir William Chambers Bagshawe, who in the early eighteen hundreds, completely remodelled the house. It was also this gentleman who stocked the fine rooms with most of the wonderful treasures it now possesses.

The tenth owner of the house, Mrs Isherwood Bagshawe, was a rather eccentric person, who did not believe at all in modern progress. Up in the house being taken over by Major and Mrs. Thornber Bagshawe in 1963, no electric light, telephone or any modern amenity was to be seen at The Oakes. Mrs. Bagshawe even closed all the rooms, the art treasures and furniture being covered over with sacking and old newspapers.

However when the old lady's health began to fail, she made the property over to her cousin, the present owner, Major Thornber Bagshawe. This gentleman and his wife, being lovers of the arts, gradually restored the interior of the house and all the lovely rooms are now again in use.

The treasures of The Oakes, to mention just a few, include Adam ceilings and fireplaces; paintings by many well known old masters, including Watts, Stubbs and Dahl; 15th century French tapestries, and Sheraton, Hepplewhite and Chippendale furniture. There is also much beautiful glass and silverware and some fine examples of Sheffield Plate.

From the terrace, designed by Sir Francis Chantrey, at the front of the house, one has vistas of green parkland, while at the rear of the house are outbuildings and stables built of warm Derbyshire stone.

The large gates of The Oakes, which bear the arms of the Bagshawe family, were made in 1722, from metal obtained upon the estate, probably from the Delves Wood area.

The house and grounds are now open to the public most weekends during the season and also on Bank Holidays.

The Nailmakers Arms

Standing back unobtrusively from what is now a byroad, but was once a main road used by coaches, is Sheffield's oldest inn, the Nailmakers Arms in Backmoor Road. Built in the year 1627, the inn's very name is a reminder of one of trades of old Norton, nail making. From when the Nailmakers Arms was built, and for many years afterwards, men made nails in the old stone cottages that were its only neighbours.

At the rear of the inn was an old brew house where the landlord brewed his own beer, a reminder of the time before the large brewery firms took control of most public houses.

The inn has unfortunately lost its ancient look, as renovations have made the exterior look almost modern. In addition the fine row of nailmakers' cottages which were adjacent to the inn have all been demolished.

The Bagshawe Arms

On the edge of the large Gleadless Valley Estate is situated the old Bagshawe Arms public house, formerly a fine country inn.

Originally this was a farmhouse belonging to the Bagshawe family and some of the old farm buildings can still be seen at the rear.

Built by the Bagshawes, with stone from the Mawfa Lane quarries, it was enlarged and renovated in 1829. Over the stable behind and to the side of the house, is a long room that was formerly the petty sessions court. A flight of stone steps outside the building lead up to the room. There is a stone in the south end of the gable which bears the initials F.W.B. (Francis Westby Bagshawe) and the date 1859.

Unfortunately the Bagshawe Arms has now become the Yate's Wine Lodge, an ugly sign has been fixed across the front exterior and modern glass doors and windows have been fitted in a side wall, all tending to spoil the beauty of this old building.

A Sheffield author, John Thomas, after a walk through Norton in 1844, called at the Bagshawe Arms and refreshed himself with a meal of pig's chap, eggs and beer. The following is his exuberant description of his visit:

'But see, our bird footed hostess, even upon the word, ushers in the needful comforts, Head of St. Swithin! what a chap is this!—Lo! here, the red and white, the streaked dainty, laid on with alternate milk and meal. What days and nights, rejoicing and grinding, had the pig which owned such jaws!—eggs fresh stolen from the covert; and beer! oh, Matthew Prior, come from Elysium, with thine own "Nut Brown Maid", and sing its praise—and thou, to whose head John Barleycorn, that most renowned of English gentlemen, talks not too loudly, come and "prie"; in this sweet drink no cunning alchemist had hand or stick,—in the copper of its concoction, no secret phial dropped; the parched barley fell into the swelling water, yielded its strength, with grateful pride, and dying kissed the ambrosial hop, which fixed its sweetness.

Now let us quaff this beer, if any were such,—and taste the ease which rural walks, light converse, and fair repletion, yield.'

The Herdings

Now incorporated in the large Gleadless Valley Estate, stands an old farmhouse, called The Herdings.

This building is of great antiquity, for the oldest part, built on Saxon foundations, is of the 13th century. The later parts of the farmhouse date from 1675, which is the date on the lintel stone.

In the time of Elizabeth the First, the farm had a windmill quite near, but this disappeared a very long time ago.

When the Gleadless Valley Estate was built, The Herdings was converted into a Youth Club, but was designed to retain most of its antiquity. The oak beams have all been preserved, and over the fireplace, in what is now the coffee bar, is the dated stone lintel which was formerly part of the external doorway.

The Grange

At the top of Bunting Nook, an ancient lane which up to quite recently had hardly altered over the centuries, stands The Grange, a house built by Joseph Offley, for his chaplain, the Rev. Daniel Lowe.

The Grange has housed many Norton worthies, including The Rev. Henry Piper, private chaplain to the Shore family of Norton Hall; Lady Ratcliffe; Mr. Cutts; Mr. Johnson; William Fisher, J.P., and John Gladwin.

Norton Grange

The house was built about the middle of the 18th century and on the plaster work ceiling in the hall is the date 1744. However, a number of alterations were made in 1852, for this date and a shield are on the mantelpiece in the dining room.

This fine old house is now the residence of Mr. and Mrs. A. Dewhurst-Smith who have lovingly restored the interior to as near its original state as possible.

The Church of St. James

The most ancient building in Norton is the lovely Church of St. James. Standing in a pleasant churchyard, at the corner of the grounds of Norton Hall, it has changed very little over the years.

Dating from Saxon times, the church was bestowed upon Beauchief Abbey between 1172 and 1176 by Robert Fitz Ranulph, Lord of Norton and Alfreton.

The interior of the church is a mixture of late Norman and Early English, with a tower arch dating back to 1180. All the plaster which covered the interior walls has been stripped away, leaving exposed the warm old stone.

An elegant feature of the church is the Blythe Chapel, which contains the alabaster memorial to William Blythe and his wife. Two of William's sons became bishops. John was consecrated Bishop of Salisbury in 1494 and Geoffrey, who was Bishop of Lichfield and Coventry, had the Blythe Chapel built and the tomb carved in memory of his parents in 1524. (see 'The Bishops' House')

The roof of the Blythe chapel is the original oak roof. The chapel is built of magnesium limestone in the Perpendicular style. On the bosses are coats of arms, the initial 'B', the letters 'I.H.S. (Jesus) and two roses. This was to show the ending of the Wars of the Roses and the union of the two rival factions.

One of the most interesting things in Norton Church is the Early English font. This is very uncommon, having carved on the east side a salamander, a kind of lizard with a humped back, twisted and forked tail, two curious little legs far back along its body, a pair of wings and two rather long ears. This animal, it is said, represents the Devil witnessing with disgust each child that is baptised to Christianity.

There are several monuments to old Norton families, including the Bullocks, Eyres, Morewoods, Gills, Clarkes, Shores and Bagshawes.

Inside the church can also be seen a clapper of the old tenor bell, used at one time for keeping open the church door. On it is inscribed the verse:

'I rang for the living, I tolled for the dead,
I gave the first greetings to those who were wed,
And still in God's house I now stand at the door,
To open its portals to rich and to poor.'

A further inscription reads:

'Clapper of the old tenor bell recast 1811,
removed from the belfry 1896.'

The Norton Parish Registers date from the year 1559. There are six parchment volumes. The first entry is the baptism of Elizabeth Greene on 30th September, 1559, in the first year of the reign of Queen Elizabeth I.

The registers contain many names of interest, including the Kirkes of Greenhill Hall (1571); the Seliokes, who settled in Norton as early as 1353; the Frechevilles of Hazelbarrow (1602); the Blythes of Norton Lees and Dronfield (1560); the Morewoods of Norton and Alfreton (1615); the Parkers (1609) and Sir Francis Chantrey (1785).

The grave of Sir Francis Chantrey, England's famous sculptor, can be seen just outside the old church porch.

At the entrance to the churchyard are the base stones of the village stocks, where local offenders of the law were fastened as a punishment for their folly.

Situated opposite Norton Church is the Rectory or 'PARSON-AGE' as it was always known. This is another of the fine buildings of Norton, built by Cavendish Neville in 1723.

Nearby, in the centre of the roadway, is a little island of grass that is all that is left of the ancient village green. Here stands the monument to Sir Francis Chantrey, an obelisk of Cheesewring granite, inscribed with the one word 'Chantrey', erected by means of public subscription in 1854. Almost 22 feet high and fixed upon steps 3 feet high, it was designed by an old friend of Chantrey's, Philip Hardwick, R.A.

This huge piece of stone was brought in one piece from Cornwall to Hull by sea, then pulled by horses across country to the little village of Norton. The monument now stands proudly to remind us of a sculptor who gave his country works of great beauty, a far cry from some of the monstrosities produced in these times under the guise of art!

St. James Church, Norton

Norton Hall

Situated at the rear of Norton Church is Norton Hall, a large mansion surrounded by parkland.

The present Norton Hall was built in 1815 by Samuel Shore, but there has been a number of earlier buildings on this site, for the hall and estates were referred to in deeds of 1166, when they were in the hands of Robert de Chauries. The hall and estates then passed through the families of Thomas de Alfreton, the co-founder of Beauchief Abbey (1226–1314); Sir William de Chawarth (1286–1348); and Blythe (1587).

From the last named, John Bullock obtained the hall in 1624 and he in turn, sold it to Cornelius Clark in 1666. However, in 1696, the estates, by bequest, came into the possession of Stephen Offley, who was High Sheriff of Derbyshire in 1716.

Stephen Offley's granddaughter, Urith, became the heiress and by marriage with the heir of Meersbrook, Samuel Shore, she brought about the ownerships of the two estates of Norton Hall and Meersbrook House into one family, the Shores. It was at this time that the existing hall was built.

The Shores were Sheffield bankers, and they possessed the Norton Hall estates until the financial crash of their Church Street bank. In 1850 the estates were sold by auction.

The new owner was Charles Cammell, the founder of the firm of Cammell, Laird and Company. It was he who added further features to the hall, which included a stately dining room, a billiards room and a colonnade.

Later Norton Hall passed through a number of hands, including Bernard Firth, a son of Mark Firth, a name well known in the history of Sheffield trade.

In recent times the hall became the annexe to the Jessop Hospital for Women, but it is now a private clinic, known as 'Beechwood'

It appears that one of the earlier halls must have been built very close to Norton Church, for a boundary wall of the churchyard clearly exhibits the remains of two ancient windows.

Sir Francis Chantrey disliked the architecture of Norton Hall, for he referred to it as 'a packing case with windows in'. It is interesting to conjecture what his reactions would have been to our modern glass and concrete buildings!

The magnificent grounds of Norton Hall are now the property of the people of Sheffield and are known as 'Graves Park', after Alderman J.G. Graves, the donor. The park was given to Sheffield in 1925. The fact that many deer used to roam freely in the grounds is commemorated in the name 'Deer Park', given to part of the upper parkland.

Norton Hall

Myrtle Springs Toll Bar

Near the top of the ancient Gleadless Road there existed a building that was one of the last operating private toll bars in Sheffield. The toll house keeper, up to as late as 1945, collected tolls from the public wishing to use the little road linking Gleadless Road with the Arbourthorne.

This private road originally belonged to the Duke of Norfolk, but about the year 1900 he sold it to Mr Wakelin of Richmond Road. This gentleman employed a Mrs Florence Darby to collect the tolls from all who used the road.

Up to the time of the toll house being demolished it was still possible to read the sign which gave the charges. These were as follows:

PRIVATE TOLL
Toll for Two Wheeled Carts........................ 2d.
Four Wheeled Carts .... 3d.
Horses, Cattle, Cyclists and
Foot Passengers .... 1d.
Pay at the Lodge.

The Bishops' House

At the top of Meersbrook Park, fronting on to Norton Lees Lane, stands the Bishops' House, one of the fairest buildings left in Sheffield.

For many years Norton Lees was the residence of a family of great note in Derbyshire, the Blythes. In 1367, John de Blythe had a grant from William de Chawarth, Lord of Norton, of a 'Messuage in Le Lyes', in the parish of Norton, with lands, etc. Later in 1485, a grant of arms was made to William Blythe and it was this gentleman who had two sons, John and Geoffrey, who became bishops and after whom the house is now called. John became Bishop of Salisbury and Geoffrey, Bishop of Coventry and Lichfield. Research and architectural evidence, however, suggests the house was built too late to have been the birthplace of the bishops.

The tomb which Geoffrey Blythe placed over the remains of his parents can still be seen in the Blythe Chapel in Norton Church. In the porch can also be seen a gravestone, the inscription reading 'Here lieth the body of William Blythe of Norton Lees, who was buried on the 9th February, in the year 1665, being in the 57th year of his age.'

The Bishops' House

Courtesy of Sheffield City Museums.

It is also interesting to note that in 1716, Mr Samuel Blythe of Norton Lees, was the dissenting minister at Attercliffe and was also buried at Norton in 1735.

The Bishops' House, which is of timber framed construction on stone foundations, was built in the 16th century, with alterations being made in the early 17th century. The date of these alterations was probably 1627, for this is the date, together with the initials 'W.B.' that are on the oak panelling in the main room.

The north end of the house is of stone and is probably late Tudor of the 17th century. There were originally large barns on the west side of the house, constructed of wood with stone foundations, but these have entirely disappeared.

After the death of Samuel Blythe in 1753, his son sold the property to William Shore. The house was then let to a tenant farmer and his labourer, and each wing made into a self-contained dwelling.

In 1886 Meersbrook Park was formed and the Bishops' House became the property of the Corporation. The house was then used as accommodation for families of the Recreation Department employees until 1974. After very extensive restoration the house was opened as a museum in July, 1976.

The Church of St. Mary, Handsworth.

The original little Norman church was probably founded by William de Lovetot, or his son Richard, sometime before 1171. Of this church only part of the chancel and the lower part of the tower remain. The tower must have been rebuilt several times, for it is recorded that in 1698, the spire was 'struck down by a ball of fire'. It was then rebuilt as a squat steeple, called by the local people 'Handsworth Stump'.

This was pulled down in 1825 and a new tower built. The church was partly rebuilt and enlargements made in the year 1852.

St. Catherine's Chapel was built about 1225 and restored in 1934. It is said to have been built by Maud de Lovetot, that prayers might be offered for the soul of her husband, Gerard de Furnival, who died on a crusade to the Holy Land.

A certain amount of rebuilding must have taken place in 1472, for in the Fabric Rolls of York of that date, we read, 'Hannesworth Church is ruinous, it is now, however, being rebuilt'.

At the rear of the church is the old Rectory and some very fine outbuildings, which were first mentioned in Henry VIII time. These buildings have foundations almost as old as the church.

They were considerably altered in the 18th and 19th centuries and are now in use as part of the Handsworth Recreational Centre.

In the churchyard, only a few yards from St. Mary's Church, is the CROSS KEYS INN. This was formerly the church house and was first used by chaplains and lay clerks attached to the church. Built probably about 1250, it eventually became a school for a century or two, then in 1800 the small building was sold to the Parish Clerk for £43. Finally it became the Cross Keys Inn as we know it today.

Bramley Hall

Situated in Bramley Hall Road, Handsworth, completely surrounded by a housing estate, is a fine building known as Bramley Hall.

Probably going back to the 12th century in its foundations, the building we see today is of the 17th and 18th centuries. The oldest part of Bramley Hall is of timber construction with stone facings.

It is probable that the first occupant of a hall on this site was Hugh de Bramley, a Norman, who in 1291 and 1292, gave most of his lands to the monks of Kirkstead Abbey.

Bramley Hall

It is recorded that some pieces of mediaeval pottery were found in a well in the grounds near the house.

The more recent part of Bramley Hall is of to Georgian period and is a very fine example of the graceful building of that era. Unfortunately a couple of stone bay windows were added, probably in the 19th century, and these tend to spoil the beautiful symmetry of this excellent Georgian house.

A striking feature of the interior is a very fine carved wooden fireplace, which reaches from floor to ceiling.

The hall is owned by Mr. J.E.C. Bond, who with loving care, keeps both the exterior and interior in perfect condition.

The Queen's Tower, Norfolk Park.

This interesting home, built to resemble a castle, was designed by Samuel Roberts in 1834. Roberts, who was a great admirer of Mary, Queen of Scots, and who was dismayed to see the Manor Lodge, where Mary had been kept prisoner, in ruins, decided to build himself a house after the style of the Lodge.

He therefore designed the house in castle form, complete with castellated turrets and a gateway with portcullis. A portion of the old wall and a mullioned window from Manor Lodge were transferred and rebuilt in the Tower grounds.

However Samuel Roberts never occupied the house, for when it was completed in 1837, he handed it over to his only son, who had married in the same year. Roberts employed as architects Woodhead and Hirst of Doncaster and he also commissioned the landscape gardener, Marnock, to lay out the grounds.

When the house was first built it was set in beautiful countryside, surrounded by fields and woods. Unfortunately it is now next door to the ultra modern Norfolk Park housing estate and is completely dwarfed by the huge towering blocks of flats.

No longer a noble residence, the Queen's Tower has been used as offices and warehouses for many years and even a petrol pump was placed incongruously in one of the castellated gateways.

In April, 1978, the house was bought by Mr. K. Oades, a director of Ballarat Ltd., a sports promotion consortium. It is now being converted into a country club and is expected to have about a dozen squash courts, with luxury changing facilities; plus dining and other club rooms.

The Manor Lodge

Situated on Manor Lane are the remains of a once great mansion, the Earl of Shrewsbury's Manor Lodge.

This very fine house was built by George, the Fourth Earl of Shrewsbury, early in the reign of Henry VIII. It was set in the midst of magnificent scenery, huge trees and parkland all around, and the little town of Sheffield nowhere in sight. No public roads, at that time, passed through the park.

The circumference of the Manor estate was about 8 miles (2,500 acres) and, it is recorded, it contained 'a thousand fallow deer and two hundred deer of antler'.

The Manor Lodge itself was an oblong building, with an inner courtyard. The house was magnificently furnished and the long gallery must have been a wonderful sight, with its tapestry, pictures, cabinets and books.

Two famous people connected with the Manor Lodge are Cardinal Wolsey and Mary, Queen of Scots.

Cardinal Wolsey was kept at the Manor by Earl George, by order of King Henry VIII, for eighteen days when he passed through Sheffield on his way to London. It is recorded that the Earl was a gentle gaoler and treated the Cardinal with great respect and kindness.

Earl George's successor was Francis, the 5th Earl of Shrewsbury. He was one of the chief mourners at the funerals of Henry VIII and Edward VI. Francis lived into Queen Elizabeth's time, eventually dying in 1560, when he was buried at Sheffield with such 'ceremony as had never before been seen in this town'.

When the Manor Lodge was in the possession of George, the 6th Earl, in 1570, Mary, Queen of Scots was imprisoned in Sheffield Castle, by order of Queen Elizabeth. George was commandered by Queen Elizabeth to act as custodian to Mary, a duty that put considerable strain on the Earl and his wife.

To give Queen Mary a little easier life, Earl George had a turret or summer house built at the Manor, where Mary could live occasionally, taking the air on the flat roof and watching the hunting of the deer.

For 14 years Mary was kept in custody, either in Sheffield Castle, the Manor Lodge or at Chatsworth House. However in 1584, Queen Elizabeth released the Earl from his duty as Mary's gaoler and the Queen of Scots was transferred to the custody of Sir Rolf Sadler and Sir John Somers.

In 1666 the spoilation of the Manor Park began with the cutting down of many of the fine old trees. It is recorded that in 1646 there stood a hundred trees worth more than £1,000. One was 13 feet in diameter near the roots and another 10 yards in circumference. When a similar tree was cut down it was reported 'that two mounted horsemen on either side of the fallen tree trunk could not see each others hats'. It was also recorded that in the Park were

Turret House, Manor Lodge *Courtesy of Sheffield City Libraries*

other trees 'a thousand worth above £6,000 and another thousand worth £4,000'.

In 1706 the Manor Lodge was dismantled, all treasures removed and the great house allowed to fall into ruin. The 8th Duke of Norfolk then built an unpretentious house in Norfolk Row, usually called the 'Lord's House', for the occasional use of himself and his agent.

The Park was then divided into farms and Duke Thomas

completed the ruination of this once beautiful district by felling the remainder of the trees.

A great gale of 1793 blew down one of the two remaining towers of the Lodge and much of the stonework was removed by the local people.

The Turret House however remained, this being the only complete structure of the Manor Lodge that exists today. In this tower is the room known as 'Queen Mary's Room', where, over the fireplace, are carved the arms of the Shrewsburys. This small room, where it is very likely Mary, Queen of Scots, was imprisoned, has also a decorated plaster ceiling and a stained glass window.

In the grounds near the Turret House is a stone coffin, considered by some to be the coffin of Lord Furnival, the founder of Sheffield Castle. For many years the stone coffin was used as a pig trough on a nearby farm. Unfortunately the stone lid has completely disappeared.

Though the Turret House has been completely renovated and a stonemason is constantly employed to preserve the ruins of the Manor Lodge, one is appalled to think how this once beautiful park was devastated. A large housing estate now surrounds the Lodge and our only reminder of the ancient Sheffield Park is the name given to the area – the Park District.

A brief list of other Sheffield Buildings, Past & Present, of Historic & Architectural Value.

Sheffield Castle.

First constructed of wood about 1150. Destroyed in 1266 during the Barons' rebellion. Rebuilt in stone in 1270 by Thomas de Furnival. Demolished in 1648 by order of Parliament.

Shrewsbury Hospital

First built near site of present Sheaf Market in 1665. Demolished in 1827, when new Shrewsbury Hospital was erected in Norfolk Road.

Town Hall

First built at the south east corner of the Parish Church yard in 1700. Second Town Hall built in 1808 at the corner of Waingate and Castle Street. (Now Crown Courts). Third Town Hall built in 1896 at corner of Pinstone Street and Surrey Street. Extensions added in 1923. Extended again in 1977.

Cutlers' Hall

Three have existed on same site. First one built 1638, second one 1725 and third and present one, 1832. Extended in 1860.

City Hall

Built 1934, in style of 20th century Classical revival. The architect was E. Vincent Harris.

Gas Offices

Built in 1874. Served for many years until the modern block was built at corner of Church Street and Fargate.

Head Post Office

Situated in Fitzalan Square. Opened on 4th July, 1910. Architecture is of the Renaissance style, with large classic columns.

Cambridge House

Built 1867. Situated in Division Street. Built in the style of a Venetian palace.

Lyceum Theatre

Opened in 1897. Interior now 'listed' as being of architectural interest. Future uncertain.

Carver Street Methodist Church

Built 1804. Architect was W. Jenkins. Large brick building.

Midland Bank, Church Street

Built in 1838. Enlarged and altered in 1878. Architect was Samuel Worth. Has row of giant columns from ground floor level.

Upper Chapel, Norfolk Street

Built 1700, altered 1848. Brick building with stone facade.

St. Marie R.C.Church, Norfolk Row

Built 1847. Architects were Weightman and Hadfield. Alterations made in 1874. Style is Geometrical to Decorated.

William & Glynns Bank, Church Street

Built 1867. Architects were Flockton and Abbott. Has coupled columns of Aberdeen granite.

Education Offices, Central Schools, Firth College, etc. Leopold Street

Firth College opened 1879. Central Schools and Offices are of 1880. Grammar School of 1876. Pupil Teachers' Centre of 1899. Firth College is in Classical style, while most of the other buildings are in the style of the Renaissance.

Victoria Hall, Norfolk Street

Built 1908. Architect was W.J. Hale. Is of brick with stone dressings.

Kemsley House, High Street

Built 1916. Architects were Gibbs, Flocton & Teather. Has tower with concave sided top. Usually called the Telegraph & Star Building.

Central Library & Graves Art Gallery, Surrey Street.

Opened in 1934. Architect was W.G. Davies. Built in Renaissance style.

Crucible Theatre, Arundel Gate

Opened 1971. Sheffield's most modern theatre. Designed by Renton Howard Wood Associates of London. Constructed of concrete and glass in irregular shapes.

Town Hall

City Hall

Meersbrook House

United Reformed Church, Norfolk Street

Very modern brick built church of 1971. Took the place of the former NETHER CHAPEL, built in 1827.

Cairn's Chambers, Church Street

Built by Henry and Alfred Maxfield. Were related to Lord Cairn who was born in 1819 and died in 1885. He was Lord Chancellor of England in 1868, in Disraeli's government. The statue over the door is of Lord Cairn.

Buildings in the Suburbs.

Totley Hall

Built 1623. Additions of 1883 and 1953. Stone, with mullioned and transomed windows. Date Stone of 1623.

Mount Pleasant, Sharrow Lane

Built 1750, by Francis Hurt Sitwell. Connected with the Sitwells of Renishaw. Is of red brick and has stable block to the north.

Meersbrook House, Meersbrook Park

Built 1760. Was residence of Shore family.

Royal Infirmary, Infirmary Road

Opened 1797. Other buildings added from 1844. Formerly called the General Infirmary. Became the Royal Sheffield Infirmary by order of Queen Victoria.

Loxley House, Wadsley.

Built 1795 and 1826. Fine stone building with Venetian windows.

Banner Cross Hall, Ecclesall Road South.

Built 1817—20. Architect was Sir Jeffry Wyatville. Stone built and castellated. Built on site of very early hall.

St. Mary's Church, Bramall Lane

Built 1830. Architects were Joseph and Robert Potter. Perpendicular style. Was a fashionable church in 19th century. Now used as a Community Centre.

Wadsley Church, Worrall Road

Built 1834. Architect was Joseph Potter. Built in Lancet style. Has piers of cast iron.

The Mount, Broomhill

Built 1834. Architect was William Flockton. Stone built, with an Ionic giant portico of six columns carrying a pediment. Was the first home of the Wilsons of Snuff Mill fame. James Montgomery also lived at The Mount for a time.

Collegiate School

Collegiate School, Collegiate Crescent

Built 1835. Architect was John Gray Weightman. GGothic style. Part altered in 1911.

General Cemetery Buildings, Cemetery Road

Built 1836 and 1848. Architects were Samuel Worth and W. Flockton. Old Chapel with Greek Doric Portico. Offices with Greek Doric Columns. New Chapel (like a church), with west tower and spire, built by Flockton in 1848.

Botanical Gardens, Gatehouse & Pavilions

The Gatehouse, with coupled Tuscan columns was built in 1836. The group of three glass Pavilions were constructed in 1837–8.

Edward VII School, Glossop Road

Built 1840. Architect was William Flockton. The style is Classical with a pedimented centre of seven bays with eight giant

Mappin Art Gallery 1900

Courtesy of
Sheffield City Libraries

Corinthian columns on the ground floor. Has end pavilions, also with giant Corinthian columns.

Oakbrook, Fulwood Road

Built 1860. Was originally the home of Mark Firth. Italianate in style, with a tower, balustrading and a porch large enough for a carriage and horses to drive through.

Tapton Hall, Shore Lane

Built 1853, by Edward Vickers. On site of much older building belonging to Shore family.

Mappin Art Gallery, Weston Park

Built 1888. Architects were Flockton and Gibbs. A pure Ionic building. Established in accordance with the terms of the will of John Newton Mappin, who bequeathed his collection of one hundred and fifty three paintings to the city.

University, Western Bank

Built 1905. Architect was E. Mitchel Gibbs. Built of red brick, in Tudor style. The OCTAGONAL LIBRARY by the same architect added in 1911.

PART 2
SHEFFIELD'S ANCIENT SUBURBS

'On Norwood's flowers the dew drops shine and shake;
Up sluggards, up' and drink the morning breeze,
The birds on cloud—left Osgathorpe awake;
And Wincobank is waving all its trees
O'er subject town and farms, and villages,
And gleaming streams, and woods, and waterfalls.'

Attercliffe

The name Attercliffe is derived from the village 'at the cliff', the cliff in question being at the bend in the River Don just below where Christ Church used to stand. This cliff can be seen quite prominently on old drawings and paintings of the middle 19th century.

In the Domesday Survey, Attercliffe was obviously considered more important then Sheffield in that it was placed first when referring to the two places, i.e. 'In Aterclive and Escafeld . . .'

Even up to the early eighteen-hundreds Attercliffe remained a pleasant country village and in 1806 it is described as follows:

'The immediate surroundings are those of rural beauty and it's scenery of hill and dale, of wood and water, are of a most pleasing character. The clear flowing Don is well stocked with a variety of fish and on both sides of the river are large and magnificent trees. The village is studded with plantations and orchards, and fruit trees overhang the footpath in many parts of the main street.'

Later in 1860, Ralph Skelton, who lived in Attercliffe from 1815 to 1877, wrote, 'There was no prettier place for miles around than Attercliffe, fine houses, Milner's, Huntsman's, Skelton's, the Vicarage, New Hall, Dr. Shaw's, all finely wooded, made a picture difficult to match. Pen and pocket knife makers were busy in their little workshops, Coe and Lister, the Casgoignes, the Millars. The shops were small and country like, the canal banks picturesque, the railway new, several farms and waving crops.'

At this period the Duke of Norfolk was the lord of the manor, but one of the principal landowners was the Earl Fitzwilliam. Most of the people were engaged in agriculture, pen and pocket knife manufacture and the steel trades.

The first place of worship to be built at Attercliffe was the small

Chapel of Ease situated in Hill Top Cemetery. This historic chapel, built in 1629, with the aid of Stephen and John Bright of Carbrook, still stands today. Unfortunately it is in a shocking state of neglect and no attempt looks like ever being made to restore this ancient building.

In 1826 Christ Church was built as a place of worship for the rapidly expanding population. This was destroyed by enemy bombing during World War II.

The first school was the Town School built in 1779, this building subsequently being converted into almshouses. Later followed the Council schools, such as Newhall in 1873, Attercliffe in 1874 and Huntsman Gardens in 1884.

Most of old Attercliffe has long since disappeared. In the eighteen hundreds one of the landmarks of the area was an old windmill with a large chimney as its neighbour. The only reminder of the windmill today is a little lane bearing its name. The chimney was demolished after it became dangerous and started swaying in high winds.

Practically all the ancient mansions are now just memories, including the Old Hall, the New Hall and Carlton House.

New Hall was a large, brick house erected by John Fell, who amassed considerable wealth at the nearby iron works. His wife bequeathed the hall and estate to the Swallow family and after they ceased to live there, it was occupied by John Sanderson. When he died, the Swallows sold the estate complete to Hunt and Company, who at great expense, converted it into pleasure gardens and sports ground.

Many folk living in Sheffield would take a horse drawn charabanc trip to Attercliffe to visit the famous Newhall Pleasure Grounds. In fact, our grandparents and great-grand-parents considered it was an ideal way to spend a day's holiday!

On the estate there was a cricket ground, a racecourse, a bowling green and a maze. There were gardens with beautiful lawns, and 'lovers' walks' shaded by large trees and decorated with statues, alongside the River Don. The river hereabouts was placid clear water and suitable for boating and fishing. On the east side of the grounds was a large lake, which served as a foreground to pictorial representations of fine cities. In the evenings musical concerts were given and the day's events usually finished with a large firework display.

There is a glimpse of the past in the name 'Salmon Pastures'. This was originally a large stretch of sandy ground alongside the Don near Attercliffe Bridge, where salmon used to spawn.

At the time of the Sheffield Flood a cottage existed on the far end of Salmon Pastures which was occupied by an old lady named

Attercliffe Common – 1792

Hutchinson. How she managed to escape death during the flood was a miracle, for the cottage was shaken to its foundations by the mighty weight of water and by colliding timbers and wreckage.

All around her humble abode swirled the bodies of people drowned in the flood, but luckily she managed to keep her head above water and she was rescued about midday the following day.

Broughton Lane, just off Attercliffe Common, takes its name from Spence Broughton.

It appears that on 9th February, 1791, Spence Broughton, once a wealthy Lincolnshire farmer, and his companion, John Oxley, held up the Sheffield and Rotherham Mail and stole the post bags, which had inside, among other letters, a bill of exchange for £123 payable to Joseph Walker of Rotherham.

Both the robbers were caught in October of the same year and were tried at York.

They were both sentenced to death, but Oxley somehow managed to escape. Broughton was executed at York Tyburn on Saturday, 3rd April, 1792, and in the grey dawn of the following Monday morning his body, which had been brought back to Sheffield, was hung in chains on a gibbet near the scene of the robbery.

This event created great public interest and for the next few days the road between Sheffield and Rotherham was crowded with a moving mass of people anxious to view the wretched spectacle of the body on the gibbet.

One person, horrified and broken hearted at the sight, was the wife of Spence Broughton, who sat at an upstairs window in the nearby Arrow Inn, weeping bitterly.

The bones of the mail robber hung on the gibbet for thirty-six years, until they crumbled and dropped from the chains. Later Henry Sorby of Woodbourne Hall, bought the land on which the gibbet stood and he had the post sawn down and removed to his coach house.

For many years afterwards, small carved ornaments, said to be made from the gibbet post, were sold at the local public houses.

John Oxley, the escaped prisoner, also met with a gruesome end. His body was found on Loxley Moor in February, 1793, just two years after the robbery.

One of Attercliffe's most colourful and interesting characters in the late 19th and early 20th century, was William Law, a shoe maker.

In 1840 Mr. Law opened a shop in Attercliffe Common, but moved to 743 High Street (now Attercliffe Road) in 1848. Here he made and sold many varieties of clogs, boots and shoes.

Fifteen years before his death he had a coffin made for himself and this he used to keep at the back of the shop. He made good use of the coffin by always having it full of bottles of brandy, whisky, gin, rum and elderberry wine, which he would give to all and sundry, postman, policeman or dustman.

He lived at his shop until he was 80 years old, then, the year being 1902, he moved to one of his own houses, No. 147 Worksop Road. He owned seven houses in that road and four in Darnall Road. On the front of one of these houses he placed the following inscription:

'Law bought it,
Law built it,
Law gave it away.
Short was my stay
In this frail world,
All's but a seeming laughter,
Therefore mark well
Thy words and ways
For thou comes posting after.'

A rather grim warning to all who passed by!

On another of his cottages was the inscription:

'What faults you see in me
Strive to avoid.
Search your own hearts.
You'll be well employed.'

At the east end of Attercliffe Common is CARBROOK, a name of Saxon or Celtic origin meaning a marshy or meadow stream. The Carr brook ran behind the old Pheasant Inn in the 18th century.

Outstanding here is Carbrook Hall, (see part I) the ancient home of the important Bright family. Now a public house, there still exists inside a beautiful oak panelled parlour, with a carved mantelpiece and moulded plaster ceiling all of 1623, the date when this part of the hall was built.

Tinsley

The name is derived from the old English 'Tingas—Leah' meaning 'Field of Council'.

In the Domesday Book it is called Tirneslawe and Tineslawe,

and belonged at that time to Roger de Busli. The first lord of Tinsley was John de Busli, Roger's father. After the De Buslis, the lordship of the manor passed to the De Tinsleys and from them to the De Wentworths, ancestors of the Fitzwilliam family.

The immense woods which then formed a part of Tinsley Park seem to have been, in Norman times, the refuge of a band of outlaws. One record tells of 'Roger de Presteman, an outlaw of Tyneslawe'.

In 1455 there was a grant by which 'Richard Wood, bailiff of Sheffield and William Swyft, of Tinsley, gave to John Hyne, of Sheffield, half a toft, built upon, and lying near Water Lane'. This William Swyft belonged to the family from which sprang Dean Swift, the famous author of *Gulliver's Travels*.

In 1732 the River Don was made navigable to a point just below Tinsley and from there a good turn-pike road was constructed right through to Lady's Bridge at Sheffield. In course of time, the river from Tinsley was connected to Sheffield by a canal, the Sheffield and South Yorkshire Navigation. This was opened for

Piper House — 1860

From an Oil Painting by the Author

traffic in 1819. The opening ceremony gave the people of Sheffield, Atrercliffe and Tinsley, a gala day and all the great men of the town travelled to Tinsley to join the fleet which was to enter Sheffield.

There were eleven vessels altogether, led by one bearing the name 'Industry' and this boat was equipped with a band, guns, flags and bunting.

When the fleet arrived at the Sheffield Docks, the event provided an excuse for unbridled feasting and speech making. There were dinners in all the taverns of the town, the principal one being at the Tontine Inn, where the Earls of Surrey and Fitzwilliam led the gentry in a feast lasting several hours.

From that time, boats being able to go right into the centre of Sheffield gave rise to a common saying by mothers to their children when asking for gifts, 'Why lad (or lass),' they would say, 'you mun stop till mor ship lands at t'bottom o' Park hill an' then ar'l ge' it thee!'

Now, unfortunately, by a great lack of foresight, the canal, a highway along which thousands of tons of goods could be borne, economically, in almost complete silence and without poisonous fumes, had been closed down. Attempts are however, being made at the time of writing, for the future use of the canal as a marina for fishing and pleasure cruising.

But to return to Tinsley, a small school was erected in 1750, chiefly supported by money from the Earl Fitzwilliam.

There was considerable excitement in the village in 1798, when a man named Hollingworth, together with a friend, broke into a shoe-maker's shop and stole a quantity of leather and hides. In a struggle with the owner, Hollingworth lost his hat and in his haste to escape he picked up a hat belonging to the shoemaker.

Later police managed to trace Hollingworth, and through him, his companion, because of the hatter's name on the band inside the hat he had left behind in the shop.

At their subsequent trial both men were sentenced to death and hanged!

In the late 18th and during the 19th century, industry gradually took over the area and Tinsley lost all its pleasant rural aspects, eventually becoming known just for its collieries, iron, steel and wire works.

Darnall

Formerly a small village on the Worksop road, the name derives from 'Derne Halh', meaning a secluded nook of land. Darnall was not mentioned in the Domesday survey and although there existed a family called De Darnall, their name is not mentioned in a list of the gentry of Henry III's reign. However, in 1641 William Spencer of Attercliffe Hall acquired the manor and this descended entire to his lineal heir, William Spencer of Bramley Grange.

In the eighteen-sixties Darnall was inhabited for most part by farmers and persons employed in the coal mines. The principal owners of this small manor were now the Chappell and Staniforth families.

The Staniforths built a hall in the centre of the village in 1723, which has long since been demolished. After the Staniforths, the house became the residence of Henry Howard, the father of the Duke of Norfolk. Later, in 1845, the hall was turned into a private lunatic asylum, but afterwards, became a private residence again.

One of Darnall's sons was William Walker, who died here in the year 1700. Walker is reputed to be the executioner of King Charles I.

In the records of York Castle for the year 1775, we read of one 'John Vickers, of Attercliffe, who was charged with robbing John Staniforth, of Darnall, of 3/6d (17½p), a sack containing horn for knife scales, a leg of mutton, 6 lb of sugar, and some flax. For this and for stealing from John Murfin, 3½d (1½p) in copper, a bad shilling, a breast of mutton and ½ lb of butter, he was hanged this same year'.

The Church of the Holy Trinity was built in 1840 and in 1855 a small hospital was rebuilt by the Staniforth family, who allowed the inmates 21/– (£1.05) yearly, together with a supply of coal. The first council school, in Darnall Road, was opened in 1875.

Just outside the village stood Captain Jeffcock's fine country house, High Hazels. Nearby was an ancient cricket ground belonging to Mr. Vickers, where many great matches were played.

Many of the colliers of the village kept greyhounds and in 1874 one of these colliers took his dog, which he valued at £40, to the veterinary surgeon. The miner told the vet that the greyhound 'was not reight' and would not eat her food. On being asked on what he fed the dog, he was told that each week she was given two nice legs of Welsh mutton and in between, fresh eggs and wine, sometimes sherry and sometimes port!

The collier earned about 50/– (£2.50) a week and his wife and children had to be content with scraps so that the greyhound might be well fed!

Darnall, like Attercliffe, has lost all traces of the pleasant country village it used to be and is now one of the areas of Sheffield scheduled for redevelopment.

Handsworth

The derivation of the name of Handsworth is 'Hand's Worth', meaning the enclosure round a homestead belonging to Hand. The village is mentioned in the Domesday Book as 'Handeswrde', the value at that time being 40/– (£2.00).

Before the Norman Conquest a lord of Danish descent, called Torchil, held the manor. Later Handsworth, with many other vast tracts of land, was given by William the Conqueror, to his half brother, Robert, Count of Mortain. As with so much of the lands in this area, the district came eventually into the possession of the De Lovetots.

It was probably William de Lovetot who built the first Church of St. Mary in the middle of the 12th century. The Church House, now the Cross Keys Inn, was used by the chaplains and lay-clerks and was built about 1250. In this area there was formerly a mansion belonging to the Earls of Shrewsbury and tradition says Mary, Queen of Scots, may have stayed at this house for a short period during her imprisonment in Sheffield.

According to the census of 1811, Handsworth Parish, which convered a large area and contained villages such as Woodhouse Mill and Richmond, etc., then contained 308 houses and 1,424 inhabitants, chiefly employed in agriculture, cutlery and collieries.

Among the old buildings still standing in Handsworth the finest is Bramley Hall, (see part I) a beautiful Georgian house, kept in perfect condition by the present owner. The name of the district, Bramley, comes from the old English 'Braemel—Leah' meaning the clearing overgrown with brambles.

Nearby is Cinderhill, an old English name meaning 'the dross hill'. Here was situated a Quaker colony said to number several thousand in 1654.

There is an old story of George Fox, the Quaker leader, who was being hunted by soldiers who wished to arrest him. A friend warned Fox that the soldiers were approaching Cinderhill. Knowing that escape by running away was impossible, Fox walked down the hill to the soldiers and calmly asked the captain of the Dragoons, for whom they were looking. On being told, 'George Fox, the leader of the Quakers,' he directed the men to a spot behind the house, where he said he had seen Fox a short time before. Then while the soldiers were searching in that area, the Quaker leader made his escape!

At nearby WOODHOUSE, once a pretty village, most of the old cottages and farms have been demolished to make way for a future housing estate. The oldest cottage was at 25 Market Square and was built in the 15th century. Originally a timber framed

Farm at Crookes — 1890

house, interleaved with wattle and daub, it was stonefaced in 1656. An ancient public house, the Cross Daggers, the base of the Market Cross and the old village stocks, have been preserved.

To the south west of Handsworth was the pleasant village of RICHMOND. Here amidst the little cottages was a farmstead, Richmond Hall Farm, built in 1668. It was owned for a time by Burrows Trippett, who died in 1772 and was buried in Handsworth churchyard. The farm was demolished, along with most of the cottages, in 1966, but ancient gateposts are still standing, looking rather incongruous, in front of the modern buildings that have taken the place of the farmhouse. These gateposts are believed to have once stood at the top entrance to the vast Sheffield Park.

Brightside

Brightside means 'Brik's ploughed land' and is a very ancient village. In the time of Henry VI the name was written as Brekesherth, for in a deed of that time Thomas de Furnival gave to the monks of Worksop 5 marks yearly 'from his mills at Brekesherth'. Also at this date, John Brekesherd was a plaintiff respecting lands in Sheffield, Kimberworth, Tinsley and Brinsford

(Brincliffe). In another deed during the reign of Elizabeth I, Brightside was written as Brixard.
The Brightside Byerlow, which included Brightside, Pitsmoor and Crabtree, had just 822 houses in 1796 and a population of 2,186. However, most of the people lived quite near to Sheffield in the Wicker and Bridgehouses area.

The Duke of Norfolk was lord of the manor and in 1860 Brightside was recorded as being 'a considerable village, pleasantly situated on the banks of the Don, about 2¼ miles E.N.E. of Sheffield. The manufacture of steel, forks, etc., are the principal trades carried on here'.

The Church of St. Thomas was opened in 1854 on a site of land given by the Earl Fitzwilliam, and a small school was built midway between Grimesthorpe and Brightside in 1802. The school held a total of 65 children and was built on land given by the Duke of Norfolk. Later in 1880 Brightside Council School was opened.

Brightside today is far from 'bright'. It is mostly industrial and a huge railway goods marshalling yard covers a large area of what was once agricultural land.

Grimesthorpe

The name of Grimesthorpe comes from the old Norse and signifies 'Grim's outlying farmstead'. In Saxon times this was the manor of Grimshaw and Ulfac was the last Saxon owner. The manor afterwards passed to De Busli, then to the De Lovetots and in course of time it came into the possession of the Dukes of Norfolk.

One of Grimesthorpe's noted families were the Saundersons whose ancestors were Peers of England and Ireland, and the family from which came Robert Saunderson, Bishop of Lincoln in 1660.

In 1870 the now rather dilapidated Grimesthorpe Road was an extremely pleasant country lane and there were many lovely walks in the large surrounding woods.

The last of the ancient cottages of Grimesthorpe were demolished a few years ago, leaving only an old iron pump to remind us of the time when, as Hunter tells us, 'the village was pleasantly situated on the sloping side of Wincobank Hill, and close beneath the wood with which all the higher parts of that eminence was covered'.

On the summit of Wincobank Hill can still be seen the remains of the camp or fort constructed by the Brigantes, the British tribes who had settled in western and southern Yorkshire. The camp was elliptical in form, with its vellum and ditch enclosing an area of several acres. Within its bounds the Brigantes clustered together in huts when the enemy threatened, but during the time of comparative security they would dwell on the slopes of the hill outside.

It is probable that here at Wincobank the Brigantes attempted to defend their land from the advancing Romans, who came from the large fort they had built at Templeborough in 54 AD.

In ancient times the scenery around Wincobank was very beautiful, with huge trees covering the slopes of the hill. John Nixon of Wincobank, in the eighteen-hundreds, wrote a poem entitled 'Wincobank Hill' and though not great poetry, his verses do give us an idea of how this area must have appeared.

> 'On Nature's vast grandeurs we look with delight,
> The scene all around is a beautiful sight,
> The flowers with fragrance the air they do fill,
> These are the productions of Wincobank Hill.
> How lovely, delightful, transporting it looks,
> All around we see forests and meadows and brooks,
> Where sweet purling waters down the valleys do rill,
> These are the beauties of Wincobank Hill.'

Though all the trees were cut down, the Pitsmoor side of the hill is now beginning to be covered with young trees again. The south east side however, is now almost entirely built over with modern houses and a large rubbish tip covers the remainder.

To the west of Wincobank lies SHIRECLIFFE, a name that is very fitting, coming as it does from Scir-cliff, meaning 'a bright, steep hillside'.

Shirecliffe of 'Shiercliffe', was the ancient estate of the De Mounteney family, descendants of Sir Robert de Mounteney, grandson of Maud de Lovetot, in the time of Henry III.

The seat of the De Mounteney's was Shirecliffe Hall, a fine house unfortunately demolished in the early eighteen-hundreds.

Lying along the banks of the River Don, at the foot of the hill where stood Shirecliffe Hall, is NEEPSEND, a name that probably means 'the house of the water spirit'. This was once a very small country hamlet where there existed a corn mill built in 1795.

Neepsend is now completely industrialized and all the once rural area is covered with works and factories of various trades.

Pitsmoor

Originally called 'Or-pits', the name means the pits from which ore was obtained. Except for these pits, the area was mostly agricultural or thick woodland.

Some of the large woods in the region of Pitsmoor, all in the 19th century belonging to the Duke of Norfolk, who was also lord of the manor, were Wincobank Wood, Hall Carr Wood, Burnt Greave, Great Roe Wood, Shirecliffe Park and Cook Wood. In the Spring most of these woods were richly carpeted with bluebells, wild anemones and pansies. Most of these woods have, of course, now disappeared.

Practically all the last vestages of Pitsmoor village have vanished also, but it is still possible to see the old Toll Bar House, standing at the junction of the Burngreave and Pitsmoor Roads. Abbeyfield House can still be seen in the park of the same name, but the ancient cottages called The Pass Houses, have been demolished. Here lived some of the miners who worked in Pitsmoor Pit.

The colliery was approached by Grimesthorpe Lane, a very old country road. Here the carts were backed under chutes, down which the coal was emptied into them. The water pumped from the pit ran down a broad culvert on the side of the lane as far as the present Burngreave Vestry Hall. At this point it was joined by the Burn (or brook), which had its rise in Old Park Wood. The water ran by Ivy Cottage in Pitsmoor Road, filled a horse trough situated in the garden wall, continued across the road, then through the glen where Burngreave Wesleyan Church was built. It then crossed the road again to run down the left hand side of Burngreave Road.

In between Pitsmoor and Firvale was the hamlet of CRABTREE, which preserved its pleasant rural aspect up to a few years ago. Now many of the 17th and 18th century cottages have been demolished to make way for a modern housing estate. One pretty cottage it is still possible to see is 'Rose Cottage', built over 300 years ago.

The district between FIRSHILL and FIRVALE was often known as 'Pitsmoor Firs' and this bring to mind an extract from a poem by the Sheffield poet and ballad writer, Joseph Mather.

'Last Easter Sunday with bat, stick and trip,
To Pitsmoor Firs I did eagerly trip,
But soon got fast in a quick-set edge;
A Methodist preacher, good natured and stout,
Took hold of my shoulders and lifted me out,

And said, "Young man, take advice from a stranger,
Permit me with freedom to tell thee thy danger,
Thou art on the road to Loxley Edge!'"

To the north of Pitsmoor were the small hamlets of Southey, Norwood and Longley.

Mulehouse Road, Crookes — 1890

SOUTHEY was the home of the Twybell family as early as 1610. James Twybell was an important man, holding office in the Earl of Shrewsbury's household. In a survey of 1637, he is shown as 'holding at will a tenement called Southall (Southey) and lands at a yearly rent of £20.'

Up to the early nineteen-hundreds Southey remained a quiet little village, but eventually the Sheffield Corporation built a large housing estate there and now not one vestage of the old Southey remains.

LONGLEY derives its name from 'Lang-Leah' meaning a long clearing. This also is now a large housing estate, with very few buildings left to remind us of previous days.

Raisen Hall, a fine 17th century building, that was situated on the south side of Herries Road, was demolished many years ago. First a cinema and now a supermarket has taken its place.

At SHIREGREEN, a name meaning the 'bright meadowland', there existed one of the oldest farmsteads in that area, Crowder House. This building was mentioned in deeds of 1402 when Julian Wilkinson left the house and estate to his son. In the eighteen hundreds it was converted into a modern residence by Bernard Wake of Sheffield, all the interior fittings being skilfully preserved. The house and fine oak panelling, oak doors and leaded windows.

The cottages that made up most of Shiregreen were called the Bell Houses and the Hatfield Houses, hence the names, Bellhouse Road and Hatfield House lane.

In the middle nineteenth century most of the inhabitants were either farm workers or fork makers.

An interesting cruck barn, probably built by Norman monks eight hundred years ago, can be seen at OAKS FOLD, a former little hamlet, at the entrance to Concord Park. The front wall of the barn, which was in danger of collapse, was rebuilt by the Sheffield Corporation a few years ago. Inside the barn can be seen the wonderful old crucks and even part of the daub and wattle filling.

To the south of Shiregreen, near Firvale, lies OSGATHORPE, an old Norse name meaning 'Osgar's outlying farmstead'. Here existed Osgathorpe Cottage, a house built on the site of a much older building. The Wake family were owners of much of the land in this area from 1750 to 1900. Most of Osgathorpe was built over in the nineteenth century.

BURNGREAVE derives its name from 'Burn', meaning a stream, and 'Greave', a grove.

Where Brunswick Road now runs, near Grimesthorpe Road, was the upper part of a lane called Tomcross Lane. This was a dark and lonesone spot overhung with tall trees and skirting the grounds of Burngreave House.

Here, in 1848, a tobacconist named Riley, who had a shop in Fargate, was murdered one night on his way home. His watch was afterwards found in a turnip field just below the Tea Garden Cottage. This house had a very pleasant garden, with leafy arbours, seats and tables. A little lane called Tea Garden Terrace still exists to remind us of this once delightful spot.

Wadsley

Wadsley got its name from the Old English 'Wadde's Leah', meaning Wadde's forest clearing.

Before the Norman Conquest, the owner was a Saxon lord called Aldene, but at the time of the Domesday Survey all his estate, like so many others in the north, was just wasteland.

The district then became the seat of the De Wadsleys, the first being Roger, who lived at the same time as Ralph, the first lord of Ecclesall.

In 1307 we find that Robert de Wadsley was then lord, for at this time Edward I granted him 'a market, on a Friday, at his manor at Rotherham, and a fair there for three days'.

During the time of Henry VI, Edmund de Wadsley held the manor, from the Earl of Shrewsbury, as the fourth part of his knight's fee.

It appears that the ancient owners of Wadsley Hall were accustomed to entertain twelve men and their horses every Christmas for twelve days and that at their departure each man was expected to stick a large pin or needle into the wooden mantelpiece over the fireplace.

Wadsley Hall is still in existence, although it was much altered by George Bamforth in 1722. Many famous and interesting people have had possession of this historic house, including the 6th and 7th Earls of Shrewsbury, the Dukes of Norfolk, the Creswick family and Sir John Fowler, the designer of the Forth Bridge.

Near to Wadsley Hall was Dykes Hall, a fine house rebuilt by John Fowler in 1852.

At what is now called Wadsley Bridge was a ford across the Don for cattle and carts, with a row of stepping stones, known as the Lepping Stones, for pedestrians. Later a wooden bridge was built and there are bills for repairs to this bridge dated 1716, 1748 and 1762. A stone bridge was built to replace the wooden structure in 1777.

A number of ancient cottages still exist in the Wadsley area, but these are being destroyed at an alarming rate.

Lepping Stones – 1770

A directory of 1862 shows a large population of Wadsley as being employed in the manufacture of pocket knives, the remainder being mostly farmers, shoemakers and tailors.

To the west of Wadsley village stands Loxley House, a fine three storied stone building of 1826. The house is used at the present time by the Sheffield Sea Cadets.

On Loxley Edge, in the year 1783, a man called Frank Fern, murdered in the course of robbery, a jeweller who was passing over the common. Fern was captured the following evening and later at his trial he was found guilty and executed. His body was then hung in chains on a gibbet fixed near the scene of his crime and it was not until Christmas day, 1797, fourteen years later, that the skeleton fell from the chains.

As late as 1810 the gibbet post was still standing on Loxley Edge and it is said that should anyone venture over this waste at midnight, he or she will hear, above the wailing of the wind, the horrible clanking of the gibbet chains!

To the east of Wadsley lies OWLERTON, a name deriving from 'Alor-tún', meaning a farmstead by the elders.

The earliest lords of this district were the Creswicks, who lived at Owlerton Hall, a building that was converted into tenements and has now been demolished.

In the 18th century a well of 'holy water' was discovered which was said to have wonderful medicinal powers. The people of Sheffield made great haste to go to Owlerton to partake of this potent water and what they could not swallow on the spot, they carried away in cans and bottles!

It is also recorded that about this time there lived at the Burgoyne Arms, a giant of a man named Hales. He is said to have been 7 feet 8 inches in height and to have weighed over 29 stone.

Very little remains of the old Owlerton today, the last ancient and picturesque cottages in the Leppings Lane being demolished during 1969 and 1970.

Malin Bridge

The name Malin probably derives from 'Melum' meaning worn stones or pebbles in the bed of the river.

This area was famous in ancient times for its water wheels, which were numerous along the Loxley and Rivelin. One of these wheels can still be seen at the Old Corn Mill at the bottom of Stannington Road. This is an underflow wheel, which is rare compared with the normal type that are turned by the water flooding over the top.

Malin Bridge and all the area around suffered very badly in the

Sheffield Flood, which occurred between the hours of 12 midnight, Friday, and one o'clock in the morning of Saturday, 12th March, 1864. During this short period, the large dam at Bradfield burst its banks and 700,000,000 gallons of water poured down the valley.

A local poet described the scene after this terrible event as follows:

'From Bradfield Hills to Bradfield Dale,
Damflask and Malin Bridge,
And all along the green-bank side,
The gorge and o'er the Ridge;
From Loxley on to Owlerton,
Across and o'er Neepsend,
And down the valley of the Don,
In every turn and bend;
From Hillsbro' on to Harvest Lane,
And all the lowlands round,
Along the Wicker and its ways,
Where'er a path was found,
The huge, uproarious sea had worked
Its devastating track,
Engulfing all within its reach
In universal wreck.
Uprooted trees, logs, bales and beams.
Great heaps of brick and stone,
And mighty engines, ripped and cracked,
Like toys about were thrown;
A thousand beings homeless made,
Upon the damp ground stood,
Pale, shivering in the cold March wind,
Knee deep in slime and mud.'

The result of this terrible calamity were 798 houses destroyed, 4,357 flooded and over 270 people drowned.

HILLSBOROUGH was given its name by Thomas Steade of Burrowlee House and Hillsborough Hall. This was done as a compliment to Lord Downshire, one of his patrons. Hillsborough Hall is situated in Hillsborough Park and was built in 1779 by the aforementioned Thomas Steade. The house was sold to the Sheffield Corporation in 1892 and is now used as a branch library.

The Barracks, usually called the New Barracks, to distinguish them from ones built in 1794, a little nearer the town, are situated between the Penistone and Langsett Roads. Built in 1850 they covered an area of 25½ acres and at that time were one of the largest military depots in the country. They had accommodation for two regiments, one of cavalry and another of infantry.

The first regiment to be stationed there was the 22nd of Foot. As there was no Officers' Mess at that time, the officers used to dine at the Hillsborough Inn. It is said that the officers had a rather sadistic brand of humour in that they amused themselves by heating small coins in the fire, then throwing them to the poor children outside in the street.

The Barracks are now used for the manufacture of gravy salt and other commodities and are now known as Burdall's Buildings.

Crookesmoor

The Crookes Moor was in olden times chiefly noted for its reservoirs and racecourse.

The latter stood where now is Fulwood Road and there was a large grandstand erected by the more wealthier inhabitants of Sheffield. The races are first mentioned in 1711, and in 1713 it is recorded that the Town Trustees were 'at charges to get horses to the races'.

These were discontinued in 1781 when the land was enclosed and a few years later the grandstand was taken down. James Wills in a poem about the Crookesmoor Races, published in 1827, starts his verse by writing:

> 'A noble racecourse, formed of hill and dale,
> Grandstand and starting post fenced round with rail . . .'

It is traditionally said that any person had the right to erect a dwelling house for himself and family on waste land between the setting and rising of the sun and that if he raised smoke (i.e. lit a fire) in that period he was irremovable.

So in the year 1789, a man called Pinder built a house of sods and stones and other odds and ends, on waste ground at Crookesmoor. Starting just after sundown and working very quickly, he had his rough house built just before sunrise the following morning and by the time any people arrived on the scene smoke was pouring from the chimney!

This house became known as 'Mushroom Hall' because it sprang up in the night, and great numbers of people journeyed from Sheffield to see the 'hall' out of curiosity.

Crookes

The derivation of the name Crookes is from the Old Norse 'Krkor', meaning a nook or corner of land. An early mention of Crookes was in an inheritance from John de Crokes to Roger Myle in 1447.

Crookes started as a very straggling settlement and as late as 1790 many of the medieval open field patterns still survived in a remarkable state of preservation. Some of the present roads are named after the old fields, such as Truswell Road, Headlands Road and Drive, etc.

The first school in the village was founded by William Ronksley of Fulwood, who gave £100 'to and for the use of a school to be built or purchased in or near Crookes in the Parish of Sheffield for ever, for which 12 children of the poorer sort be chosen out of Crookes aforesaid and out of the neighbourhood thereof shall be taught to read English only'.

Later in 1794 a larger school was erected by the local inhabitants.

In the nineteenth century Crookes was regarded as one of the holiday spots of Sheffield, healthy and invigorating! Thomas Asline Ward, writing to a friend in 1855, said, 'I find that your son has taken a partner and gone to Crookes for the country air. I am sorry his wife requires it and hope her health will soon be restored.'

There was a rather amusing incident at Crookes which occurred in 1870, when the Prince and Princess of Wales came to Sheffield to open Firth Park.

All the inhabitants of the village were elated when they heard that on the day after the ceremony, the Royal couple, who were the guests of Mark Firth at Oakbrook, were to drive through Crookes in open carriages.

The villagers hurriedly put out flags and decorations and waited for the Princes and Princess to arrive.

Unfortunately when the carriages passed through, the Princess was not amongst the party. This caused great disappointment until a philosophic old lady was heard to remark, 'Well, never mind, I know 'ow it is. There was a party at Oakbrook, yer know, last night, and I've no doubt the Princess is stopping behind to help Mrs. Firth with the washin' up!'

In 1887 a Bronze Age Cinerary urn containing human bones, a small cup and a damaged bronze knife, were found in the ground near old Tinker Lane. This lane leads from the top of Crookes towards Rivelin.

Near the place of this find was St. Antony's Well, which was believed to have medicinal properties. St. Antony was the patron saint of the swineherds and of course, the neighbourhood, with its

View from Crookes – 1826

oak forests, was ideal for the feeding of pigs. The custom was that one pig from each litter was vowed to the saint.

Very little is left today of the old Crookes and many of the roads, including the main street, are now lined with brand new houses and flats.

The name of the former village of WALKLEY comes from the Old English 'Walca's Leah', meaning Walca's forest clearing.

Because the village was built on the side of a steep hill, bleak and open to the continuous winds blowing across the Rivelin, the people of Walkley, like those of Crookes, were a hardy and healthy folk.

Near where Heavygate Road now runs, was a fine house called Walkley Hall, probably built by William Rawson about 1600. The Hall was demolished by the Sheffield Corporation in January, 1926, to make way for the present housing estate.

In 1637 the area where Bell Hagg Road now is, was a large open common of about 80 acres. On this land the owners of the little farms at Crookes and Walkley, turned their cattle in the summer. The name Bell Hagg comes from the Old Norse 'Bale or Belle-Hagi', meaning a fire common.

One of the interesting buildings still standing in Walkley is the old Heavygate Inn. This was built in 1696 and has walls two feet thick. In 1896, to celebrate the 200th anniversary of the opening of the inn, a sheep was roasted in the yard and all who passed that day were given a free sandwich and a drink. It is only to be imagined that more than the usual number of people passed the 'Old Heavygate' on that particular day!

John Ruskin, the famous art collector and critic, bought a house overlooking the Rivelin valley, which he converted into a museum to house his fine collection of works of art and other objects. The collection was later transferred to Meersbrook Hall, a former home of the noted Shore family. The building that housed Ruskin's collection at Walkley, 'Ruskin House', still stands, though altered considerably when it was converted into a 'Girls' Home'.

In the year 1880 the residents of Walkley became worried by a prediction that a volcano would suddenly erupt there on a certain day. Great damage to the area was prophesied!

However, much to the disappointment of many of the people, when the time came for the eruption nothing happened and so an alternative entertainment was provided.

A man who prided himself on his sense of humour, obtained a wheel barrow, filled it with tar and set it alight. He then sent the blazing barrow careering down Blake Street, which is a very steep hill.

It needs little imagination to think of the commotion this incident caused!

The main road leading into Walkley is called Barber Road and this acquired its name from the Barber family who resided at Barber Nook House, a pleasant little cottage built in 1728, and still standing just off the main road behind the Co-operative Stores.

Nearby is an area of very fine houses and gardens called Birkendale. This name was derived from the German 'Birkenthal', meaning a valley of birch trees.

Ecclesall

The name Ecclesall probably derives from 'Hecksel-Hallr' meaning the witches' hill, or slope. That this area had association with witches and their like is shown also in Dobbin Hill, which comes from the northern word 'Dobby', meaning a goblin. And of course, nearby Endcliffe was the elf cliff or bank!

No mention of Ecclesall is made in the Domesday Book, but in the time of King John, about the time when Gerard de Furnival married the great heiress of Hallamshire, Maud de Lovetot, there appears on the scene Ralph de Ecclesall, who had settled in this district. Ralph gave much of his land to the monks of Beauchief and when he died he was buried at the Abbey.

His son was Sir Robert de Ecclesall and he confirmed his father's grants to Beauchief. Sir Robert's son was also called Ralph after his grandfather and he was also a knight of the realm. It was he who gave to Beauchief Abbey his mill on the Sheaf, from which comes the district known as the Mill Houses.

Ecclesall had a very ancient chapel built in 1046. It was a small, low building, consisting of two parts, a nave and a chancel. There was a small shed at the west end that contained a bell.

The monks of Beauchief took service in the chapel, to which there was a pleasant walk over the fields. The services were discontinued on the Dissolution and no further service was performed there until 1622. At that time the chapel was restored by the walls being rebuilt, a floor was laid in the chancel and pews set up. A pulpit, communion table and new glazed window were also installed. A small wooden steeple was erected on the chapel roof.

This chapel was the only place of worship for the people of Ecclesall until 1788. In that year a new church was built, near the old building, on a spot called CARTER-KNOLL (Carterknowle). The old chapel was then demolished.

Ecclesall Road – 1830

From an Oil
Painting by the Author

There has never been a village of Ecclesall, it has always been a scattered district. Even as late as 1723, there were only one and a half persons to the acre!

In 1796 Ecclesall contained 1,071 houses and in 1811 the population was only 6,569 people. Most of the inhabitants were engaged in agriculture, though some worked for the manufacturers of Sheffield. A number of people were employed at Wilson's Snuff Mills, which still exists just off Ecclesall Road.

Around this time the poor people of this district received £7 : 14 : 0d (£7.70) annually, the money being subscribed by several benefactors. There were also bequests for the education of poor children.

Most of the south west corner of the area, was and still is, occupied by Ecclesall Woods, formerly the property of the Earl Fitzwilliam, who was also lord of the manor.

In these extensive woods, at the Beauchief side, is a gravestone in memory of a charcoal burner who died in his cabin when it caught fire one night.

The charcoal burners or 'wood colliers' as they were known, came mostly from the east end of Sheffield. They would make and light their 'stacks' on a Sunday, so that they could have the charcoal to sell to the steel works the following Friday or Saturday, and so get paid.

The inscription on the gravestone reads:

> 'In Memory of George Yardley, wood collier, he was burnt to death in his cabin on this place OCTR 11th, 1786.
> William Brooke, salesman;
> David Glossop, gamekeeper;
> Thomas Smith, beesome maker;
> Sampson Brookshaw, inn keeper.'

The last four names of the inscription were friends of the charcoal burner and it was they who erected the gravestone. The first is probably that of the woodman who sold the wood for charcoal burning to those who wanted it; the gamekeeper must have regularly come across Yardley when on his work in the woods; the beesome maker would probably have carried on his craft close by; while the inn keeper would have been the landlord of the 'Rising Sun', a nearby public house with a very ancient history.

To the north west of Ecclesall lies Whiteley Woods, a name that is derived from 'Hwit-Leah-Wudu', meaning a bright, fair clearing.

Here was situated Whiteley Wood Hall, originally the home of the Ashton family. From them it passed to the Pegges of Beauchief, who sold it to Thomas Boulsover, the inventor of Sheffield Plate. After Boulsover died the house became the property of William Hutton, then by marriage, it passed to the Silcock family. It is interesting to note that it was a member of this family, Phoebe Silcock, who subscribed the money to build the beautiful Christ Church at Fulwood.

The name of FULWOOD comes from the Anglo-Saxon 'Ful-Wudu', meaning a wet, marshy woodland. This was, in ancient times, a vast, pasturage forest, abounding with trees of fine growth. Here Thomas, Lord Furnival granted to the canons of Beauchief Abbey 'common of pasture in his free chaces of Folewode and Ryvelingdene everywhere, sufficient for all their cattle, except goats'.

The old lords of Sheffield however, also reserved part of this domain for the pleasures of the chase and it was probably here and in Rivelin, that Robin Hood (or Locksley) made some of his first attempts at 'chasing the fallow deer'. This area lies not very far from Loxley, the legendary home and birthplace of the famous outlaw. This is borne out by the historian Dodsworth, who in 1620 wrote:

'Robin Locksley, born in Bradfield parish in Hallamshire, wounded his stepfather to death at plough, fled into the woods, and was relieved by his mother till he was discovered. Then he came to Clifton upon Calder, and became acquainted with Little John, that kept the kine. Which said John is buried at Hathershead in Derbyshire, where he hath a fair tombstone with an inscription. Little John was Earl Huntley's son. Afterwards he joined with Much the Millar's son. . . .'

To protect the deer in Fulwood and Rivelin, keepers were appointed by the lords of the manor. The head keeper was known as 'Master of the Game' and each man received the princely salary of £2 per year. However, after the time of Charles I, there was so little game left in the area that the posts of keeper were discontinued.

In 1666, which was a period when people were very alarmed at the spread of the plague, Fulwood Spa was a popular resort. This was a spring of mineral water, which was eventually covered with a building by Thomas Heaton, converting it into a 'spa'. Many Sheffield people then visited Fulwood to 'take the waters'.

The spa was situated near the ancient Fulwood Chapel, built in 1729. The stocks which formerly stood on the village green, can be seen in the small garden in front of the chapel.

There are many old buildings in the Fulwood area, the most

noticeable being Fulwood Hall, a building mentioned in deeds of the time of Henry VII.

Today most of Fulwood is a district of fine, large houses, built mostly during the Victorian period, by the rich industrialists of Sheffield. It is a beautiful area and this is reflected in some of the street names, such as 'Hangingwater', meaning a deep, slow moving stream.

One of the ancient esquire seats in the manor of Ecclesall was BANNER CROSS, a name that comes from the old French 'Baneur', meaning a standard bearer. At the time of Elizabeth I this was called the Banner Field and here was situated the home of the Bright family of that area.

When the Brights became extinct in 1748, the grand-daughter and heiress, Mary Dalton, conveyed the estate to her husband, Lord John Murray of the house of Athol. During his occupation Lord John made many improvements to the hall. However, when it came into the hands of General Murray, he practically demolished the building, and with the assistance of Sir Jeffry Wyatville, he erected the present Banner Cross Hall.

The Scottish names of many of the streets of this area reflect the influence of the Murray family, who came from Tullibardine Castle.

Sir John Murray brought with him to Banner Cross many servants and amongst them was a man called Wragg and his wife. These people were housed in the old Dove Cottages (now demolished) which stood on the site of the present Louth Road. Mr. and Mrs. Wragg had a daughter called Molly who went into 'service' and eventually came to settle down as a midwife and nurse in a little cottage at the top end of Brincliffe Edge. Molly was looked upon as a curer of all ills, so when anyone was sick, the cry was always, 'Fetch Molly Wragg!' Because of this Brincliffe Edge Road was locally known to all as 'Molly Wragg Lane'.

To the north of Ecclesall lies ENDCLIFFE, which was originally called 'Elcliffe', meaning Elf Cliff or Bank. The name is at least as old as 1333 when it was mentioned in a grant to a certain John de Elcliffe.

Dore

The name of Dore is derived from the Anglo Saxon 'Dor', meaning a door, pass or entrance into the kingdom of Mercia.

It is a very ancient village, for here in the year 829, Ecgbert, King of Mercia held a meeting with Eanred, King of Northumbria. The result of this was that Ecgbeet was declared King of all the English and the Kingdom of England emerged.

The Anglo-Saxon Chronicle from which so much of our early history is obtained, relates the incident as follows: 'And Ecgbert led an army to Dore against the Northumbrians and they offered him obediance and concord, and thereupon they seperated'. Ecgbert then became 'Our Lord of the whole English speaking race from the Channel to the Firth of Forth'.

In 1968, one thousand, one hundred and thirty-nine years after this historic event, a commemorative plaque attached to a large stone, was erected on the village green.

In ancient times the only road from Abbeydale to the village was an old pack horse lane which skirted Ashfurlong and came out at the top of the hill into what is now the main road. Even at the time of the Commons Enclosure, which took place in Dore from 1809 to 1822, there was only one road from Whirlow Bridge to Totley. This was the only cart road from Sheffield into Dore.

Though mostly agricultural land, the village was also well known for supplying coal to the lead smelters who brought their lead from all parts of Derbyshire to the smelting cupolas driven by water power. There were many water wheels in the area, a number of which powered corn mills in Ryecroft Glen, Barber Field and Old Hay.

The people of Dore were employed in various trades, including button makers, saw and anvil makers, file cutters, boot and shoe makers and of course, agriculture.

Lyn Mill, Dore – 1873

The Parish Church for this district was at Dronfield, but a small Chapel of Ease was erected at Dore, probably around 1530.

There is an amusing story relating to a man called Frank Parker who was curate of the village for some years, previous to 1836. Mr. Parker lived in Sheffield town and only came over to Dore on Sundays to take the service. On his visits he was often accompanied by a friend called Jeeves and after the service they would dine at the 'Hare and Hounds'.

It is said that if the sermon happened to drag on too long, Mr. Jeeves would go to the pulpit steps, tug at Mr. Parker's gown, and in a very loud whisper would say, 'Frank, Frank, t' goose will be ready: cut it short, man!'

The old Chapel of Ease was demolished in 1828 when the present church was built.

Another interesting character of Dore was Richard Furness, who was not only schoolmaster, but also overseer, architect, scribe, lawyer, doctor, singer, poet and surveyor. A poem describing his various talents went as follows:

'I, Richard Furness, Schoolmaster, of Dore,
Keep parish books and pay the poor;
Draw plans for buildings, and indite
Letters for those who cannot write;
Make wills and recommend a proctor,
Cure wounds, let blood with any doctor;
Draw teeth, sing psalms, the hautboy play
At chapel on each holy day;
Paint sign boards, cart names at command,
Survey and plot estates of land;
Collect at Easter, one in ten,
And on the Sunday say—Amen!'

In the 19th century Dore was still a small straggling village, with about 500 inhabitants. One of its fine old buildings was Dore Hall, which was owned by Ralph Barker in the 14th century. The hall is described as a fine mansion, with beautiful oak panelling and decorated plaster ceilings. Unfortunately the hall was demolished in 1840.

Today we find much of the old village destroyed, with modern houses, shops and schools spreading out across the once open fields.

To the south of Dore is the former hamlet of TOTLEY. It was called in the Domesday Book 'Totingelei', a name meaning a spy or watching place. 'Toting hills' are often met with in early literature, in all cases being places of defence. Totley being situated on the summit of a steep hill would be an ideal place from which to spy out the land and watch for enemy movements.

Beauchief

Beauchief was the name given by the Norman monks to the area in which they built their Abbey. It means 'beautiful headland' and refers to the delightful countryside around.

The Abbey was founded by Robert Fitz Ranulf, probably about 1183. It was dedicated to Archbishop Beckett and the Virgin Mary, and was given to the White Canons, some of whom came from Welbeck to settle at Beauchief.

The Abbey continued to function until the Dissolution in 1537, when it was surrendered to King Henry VIII.

Many of the stones from the Abbey were used to build the beautiful Beauchief Hall, situated a short distance away.

At Beauchief can also be seen a reconstructed 18th century industrial hamlet, called the Abbeydale Works. At this museum of one of Sheffield's oldest industries it is possible to trace the manufacture of steel edge tools from the raw materials to the finished product. Both the forging and grinding machinery were worked by water wheels and these have been carefully reconstructed to illustrate the working conditions of those early days.

Millhouses

As mentioned previously this name comes from the Corn Mill on the River Sheaf given by Ralph de Ecclesall to the monks of Beauchief. It was then known as the Miln Houses or Mill Houses.

In the 12th and 13th centuries the mighty forests of Barnsdale covered most the country around these parts and here lurked many bands of outlaws to hunt the King's deer. The River Sheaf had many fine trout and these must often have furnished a good meal on Fridays at the Abbey.

In the middle eighteen-hundreds there were only 23 houses and a few dilapidated file cutters' shops. There were also, at this time, seven small pits within a mile radius, in which implements used by the monks of Beauchief were found.

With the exception of the Old Mill, the Robin Hood Inn and the cottages, there were only fields and woods until one came to the 'Waggon and Horses'. This very ancient inn was probably a farmstead in its earlier days.

Abbeydale

Abbeydale derives its name from the 'dale of the Abbey' or Abbey-Dale'.

It has never been a village, but simply a valley near the River Sheaf, being up to the middle 19th century completely rural. From the Royal Hotel at the end of Highfield there were practically no houses on Abbeydale Road, with the exception of Broadfield Toll Bar, until one came to Millhouses.

A pleasant mansion later situated in the dale was Abbeydale House, built by Joseph Rodgers, founder of the great cutlery firm of that name.

Adjoining this house and estate was the Broadfield Park Estate, once owned by the Shore family and later by the Shirecliffes.

Of this latter family it was said that there was 'no holding one of the daughters'. We are not told of her misdeeds, but when she died her father was determined that she should now 'be held' if weight of stone could accomplish it. So he had her buried at Heeley Church and a large team of horses had a heavy task to drag the weighty tombstone to the churchyard to 'pin down' this lively lady!

Broadfield Toll Bar was so called because it was situated at the top end of the Broad Field, the only reminder of this field being the road of the same name. The Bar was erected in 1812, when the Abbeydale Road was constructed. A pleasant country path led from the toll bar to Little London Lane at Heeley. It was bordered by a row of fine trees and over-looked the beautiful Primrose Meadows. When this land was developed for housing, many people complained about the destruction of these trees, but, just as today, it was of no avail.

Remains of the ancient country footpaths still exist. One runs from Abbeydale Road to Chesterfield Road and the other from Broadfield Road to Little London Road. Now called 'gennels', they have been reduced to dirty, rubbish strewn passages and the once beautiful River Sheaf, over which they pass, is now a rubbish filled, polluted, vile smelling stretch of water.

Between Abbeydale and Ecclesall lies NETHER EDGE, a once rural area that was developed by George Wostenholm. Wostenholm commenced buying land in this district in 1836, until eventually he owned most of the land from Brincliffe Edge down to London Road. Upon this land, Wostenholm and Thomas Steade built the fine Nether Edge Estate, mostly detached villas in large gardens. Basing the estate on the town of Boston, Massachusetts, in America, trees were planted at the sides of all the roads, leaving a fine heritage for the occupants of the area today.

Adjoining Nether Edge was the medieval hamlet of CHERRYTREE, up to comparatively recently a beautiful oasis of little cottages on what is called Cherrytree Road. Unfortunately many of the cottages have now been destroyed.

Heeley

Heeley derives its name from 'Heah Leah', meaning a high, woodland clearing. It is first mentioned in a charter of 1343, when it was called 'Heghlegh'. In 1348 it was spelled 'Heghelegh' and in 1451 it is referred to as 'Hamelet-de-Heyle'. However in 1553, the spelling is as it appears today.

The village of Heeley nestled on the hillside around the church and green. As the village grew it split into Upper, Middle and Nether Heeley, this latter part now being better known as 'Heeley Bottom'. In the 19th century, where the unused Heeley Railway Station now stands, was a large sheet of water and horse teams bringing their loads to town would stop to drink.

Near the bridge over the Sheaf, first erected in 1567, stood the Heeley Tilt and from there a thickly wooded bank extended to the bridge at Myrtle Road. In this wood, at the beginning of the 19th century, a murder was committed, the perpetrator of which was executed at York Castle. All around this area were pasture lands and cornfields, extending across to East Bank and The Farm.

The spot near Heeley Toll Bar, commonly called 'Heeley Gates', was noted for many daring robberies. Records tell us that 'In 1839, about 8 o'clock at night, Robert Turner of Bole Hill, Norton, was stopped by five ruffians, who took his hat, umbrella and 15/– (75p) in money'. On another evening, a man called Trickett, a fish dealer, was stopped and robbed by several men of 5/6 (27½p).

Just off Gleadless Road, behind where the Shakespeare Hotel now stands, was Heeley Hall, an ancient 15th century building. All traces of this hall have now disappeared.

Many interesting field names existed in this area, including one called 'Two Days Work'. This was mentioned in a document of 1663 and obviously this must have been an exceptionally large field.

At the end of Oak Street stood a whitewashed farmhouse, surrounded by corn fields. This was demolished many years ago. In a wall that used to surround the now demolished Oak Street Church, was fixed a date stone on which were carved the initials A.I.M. and the date 1717. This stone came from a cottage which was knocked down to make way for the widening of Gleadless

Heeley, with White Lion in background — 1825

Road. The old stone, along with the wall, was destroyed by the bulldozers which completely flattened this part of Heeley during 1970.

Heeley Church was opened in 1848 and there was a school erected in 1833, endowed with lands amounting to about £20 a year.

In the churchyard is a granite memorial to J. Shortridge of Chipping House. He was the man who built the railway from Sheffield to Manchester, and who was also responsible for the Wicker Arches.

There were many wells and springs at Heeley and these are remembered in the names Well Road, Well Head Road and Springwood Road.

At the bottom of Well Road there existed a 'Catch Bar' which was erected there to prevent travellers evading the Heeley Toll Bar.

The beginning of the changes that led to the Heeley of the present day began with the draining of the Little London Dam, to make way for the Midland Railway. Then the Hardy Patent Pick Company and Sir Charles Skelton's shovel works opened up new fields of industry, bringing with them an influx of workers. These workers required to live close at hand and so houses were built all around the works. Street after street gradually thrust over the hillside and to meet the requirements of the new population, enterprising shopkeepers opened up businesses all along the main road.

To the south east of Heeley was the straggling village of GLEADLESS, a name which comes from the Old English 'Glida

Red Lion Inn, Heeley — 1876

Leah', meaning a kite clearing in a wood. All the farms and most of the cottages of Gleadless have now disappeared, modern houses and shops taking their place.

The GLEADLESS VALLEY, formerly a beautiful stretch of open countryside and woodland, extending from Heeley to Norton, now houses the 'show estate' of Sheffield. Unusually good planning of the streets and houses on the contours of the valley has preserved a number of open spaces and trees which would otherwise have been destroyed.

To the north east of Gleadless lies HOLLINSEND, formerly a stragging hamlet of small cottages and farms. Here existed two of the oldest cottages in the Sheffield area. Built in the 15th century, these picturesque homes were, a few years ago, stated to be 'unfit for human habitation' and demolished. Referring to the buildings being unfit for human habitation, it should be noted that one of the cottages was occupied by the Crouch family for many generations and ALL the members of that family died at a ripe old age. The last tenant was Mr. Joe Crouch who died in 1962 at the age of 82!

To the east of Hollinsend is situated HACKENTHORPE, a name meaning 'Hachen's outlying farmstead'. In 1860 this was a village of sickle manufacturers, 30,000 dozen being made each year. One of the largest employers of labour in this area being Thomas Staniforth of Darnall.

Nearby is BIRLEY SPA, named after a spring of mineral water that was found very beneficial to health. Earl Manvers, the owner of the district, 'empowered a committee of four gentlemen to erect a large establishment of seven baths, for the use of the public, in 1843'. As it was pointed out at the time, the Spa was 'situated in a sylvan and rural glen, entirely surrounded by romantic hills, tastefully laid out and planted'.

Now, of course, Birley Spa is surrounded by a large, modern housing estate.

To the south of Heeley is MEERSBROOK, a name derived from the stream called the Meers Brook that runs down from Norton Lees until it meets the River Sheaf at Saxon Bridge, Heeley. The Meers Brook means a 'boundary brook' and it and the Sheaf formed part of a frontier line between the ancient Kingdoms of Northumbria and Mercia. Up to comparatively modern times this brook was also the boundary between Yorkshire and Derbyshire.

At the top of Meersbrook Park, at NORTON LEES, is one of Sheffield's oldest houses, the 'Bishop's House'. Built probably in the 16th century, it acquired its name from the two bishops of the Blythe family, John and Geoffrey.

Up to the middle of the nineteenth century the road from Meersbrook to Woodseats was completely rural and very sparsely populated. On each side of the road was Smithy Wood, which extended from the River Sheaf to the top of Scarsdale Road, formerly called Green Lane.

Woodseats

Woodseats or Norton Woodseats was originally called 'Wodesettes' and its inhabitants in ancient times were mostly occupied in assisting the monks of Beauchief Abbey with their agriculture.

Most of old Woodseats was clustered around a farmstead near a little narrow lane called The Dale. All the old cottages and the farm have been demolished during the last few years.

Other cottages existed along what is now Chesterfield Road and near the Cold Brook, opposite Cobnar Road. Here also, was a farm belonging to a man called Jonathon Booth, and it is recorded that John Wesley stopped and preached a sermon here, as he passed through Woodseats in the year 1753.

The little school that still stands at the bottom of Cobnar Road was erected by Charles Cammell in 1861. Charles Cammell lived at Norton Hall and the estate and grounds of this fine house are now known as Graves Park. This beautiful park extends from Norton to Woodseats and covers an area of two hundred and six acres. The park acquired its name from Alderman J.G. Graves, who presented the estate to the City in 1925.

The original Big Tree Inn, so called from the tree growing in the forecourt, was a stop for the horse drawn coaches on their three day journey to London. The present inn is the second one on this site, as also is the tree that grows in front.

Norton

The name of Norton is derived from 'Nord-Tún', meaning the north farmstead.

It was first mentioned in the will of Wulfric Spott, who appears to have been an officer attached to the court of King Ethelred in 1002.

The Manor of Norton at the time of Edward the Confessor, belonged to Godeva and Nada. Afterwards it passed through the families of De Busli, Fitz Ranulph, Chaworth, Ormond, Dynham, Babington and others, until it came into the hands of the Offleys, from whom it passed to Samuel Shore, of Norton Hall.

The old Norton village was a picturesque place, described in one record as follows: 'Norton is interesting and pleasant, the cottages are generally plain, but being embosomed in gardens, festooned with roses, or overhung with trees, present an unusual air of comfort and repose.'

The lovely church of St. James, dating from Saxon times, was bestowed upon Beauchief Abbey by Robert Fitz Ranulph, Lord of Norton, between 1172 and 1176.

An elegant feature of this church is the Blythe chapel, built in 1520, in which is the tomb of the Blythe family. The Blythes lived in the previously mentioned Bishop's House at Norton Lees.

When restorations were made to the church in 1882, a memorial stone dated 1674, which lay under the altar adjoining the east window, was found to tell the usual story of Barbara Lee. It appears this good lady was buried under or near the fireplace, which was then situated on the site of the altar. The body was buried upright in a perpendicular hole, with the fireplace over the head. It is said that this may have been done for a particular reason, but probably there was no room to lay the coffin in the usual position.

Both in the church and in the churchyard are many monuments to notable Norton families, including the Bullocks, Eyres, Morewoods, Gills, Clarkes, Shores and Bagshawes. The grave of Sir Francis Chantrey can be seen just outside the old church porch.

Many of the grave stones have been lost or broken quite recently in an unnecessary 'tidying up' of the churchyard. One old stone

Machon Bank — 1873

had the following inscription in memory of a blacksmith who lived and worked near the top of Meadowhead:

'Mark Tyzack, of Four Lane Ends,
Blacksmith, Buried in 1795.
My scythe and hammer lies reclin'd;
My bellows too, have lost their winde;
My iron is spent, my steel is gone;
My scythes are set, my work is done;
My fire extinct, my forge decay'd;
My body in the dust is laid.'

Near the church, on a small piece of grass that is all that is left of the village green, stands on obelisk of Cheesewing granite, a memorial to Sir Francis Chantrey, erected by public subscription in 1854.

In the 17th and 18th centuries, fine houses were erected in and around the village, most of these still standing today. These include Norton Hall, the Parsonage, Norton Grange and the Oakes.

The only public house, complete with a large bowling green, was at MAGATHAY, (wrongly called MAUGERHAY today), a picturesque hamlet that clustered around the inn. Here was an ancient field with the unusual name of 'Plackling Magatha'. The name came from the Anglo Saxon 'Placke', meaning an open space and the second part is obviously a shortened form of Magathay.

At HEMSWORTH nailmakers lived and worked in their small

cottages around an inn, called the Nailmaker's Arms. The licence for this public house was granted in 1626. Nearby was a farmstead that later became the Bagshawe Arms and it is interesting to note that in the 19th century an outbuilding of this public house was used as the Petty Sessions Court, held every second Wednesday of the month.

Among the many old superstitions adhered to by the farmers of this area was one that required a pig's hock being hung up in the farmhouse. This piece of bacon had to be white-washed everytime the house was whitewashed and this was believed to protect the cattle from disease!

To the south of Norton Church was the small hamlet of JORDANTHORPE, a name of Danish origin meaning Jourdain's outlying farmstead. Here, Sir Francis Chantrey, one of England's most famous sculptors, was born in 1781.

Of the old buildings, only Jordanthorpe Hall, Chantrey's Cottage and Jordanthorpe Hall Farm remain.

Cinderhill Lane, on the side of which all these buildings stand, was, up to a few years ago, extremely beautiful. Here it was possible to wander between hedgerows of wild flowers, to see for miles across unspoiled countryside and to have one's ears filled with birdsong. Occasionally from the nearby woods of Hazlebarrow could be heard the barking of a dog fox and hares could be observed scampering across the fields.

However, in 1969 the bulldozers arrived, the ancient hedgerows were ripped from the ground and within a few months modern houses were covering the scene. Cinderhill Lane then became just another piece of suburbia. But worse was to come, for a giant ugly electric sub-station was built in the fields behind the old farm!

Though Norton managed to keep its rural aspect longer than most of Sheffield's suburbs, the tentacles of development are now gripping it tightly and modernity is quickly taking over. The square glass boxes of modern schools cover the corn fields, the cottages of Magathay have been reduced to rubble, huge housing estates creep over the grazing lands toward Hazlebarrow and even the beautiful Oakes Park is threatened by the aforementioned motorway.

> 'To Norton, then, farewell,
> The homes, the church upon the village green,
> Old thoughts that circle like the birds of even'
> Round the grey tower. Soft, sweet regrets, like sunset
> Lighting old windows with gleams day had not,
> Ghosts of dead years, whispering old names
> Through the grass grown pathways and age-old trees.'

PART 3

STORIES, LEGENDS & ANECDOTES OF OLD SHEFFIELD

'Listen and I'll tell you stories
Of ancient Sheffield and its glories,
Of characters that are long dead,
Of ghosts and gibbets and a silver bed!'

The Life and Times of Joseph Mather

Joseph Mather was born in 1737, in 'Cack Alley', a jennel which led from Lambert Street to Westbar Green. As a youth he was apprenticed to the file trade in the small works of Nicholas Jackson of Shemeld Croft.

Joseph was only small, but rather wide in breadth and for most of his younger days he belonged to the Methodists. From them he acquired a good knowledge of the Bible, from which he frequently quoted.

To earn a few extra coppers, Mather, throughout his life, composed ballads, which he sold in the streets and at public houses. Usually when selling his songs, he would ride seated the wrong way round on a grinder's donkey and sometimes on the back of a young bull. Should it start to rain he would steer the animal into the nearest alehouse.

Though Mather's moral character was reasonably good, he was easily led astray, and quite often he would finish up in the old gaol in Pudding Lane, (now King Street). This was a debtor's gaol, of only two cells, one for each sex. Sheffield folk could be sent there for owing as little as sixpence!

The last years of Mather's life were spent in sickness and poverty. His house was now in Pond Hill and when he died in 1804, at the age of 67, he was buried in St. Paul's churchyard.

It was fitting that the funeral service should be performed by the Rev. Alexander Mackenzie, for during his life Mather had many times satirised the parson under the title of 'Old Crow'.

The ballads written by Mather symbolized the terrible conditions under which most Sheffield people lived, as the following extract clearly illustrates:

'Poverty, that vile tormentor,
Keeps me in strong bonds confined;
Fortune quits me at a venture
Since I've got a generous mind,
Rags disguise me, friends despise me,
Bums and lawyers catechise me,
All against me seem combined.
Chorus.
Wearied bones, despised and daunted,
Hungry guts and empty purse,
Hung with rags, by bailiffs haunted,
Prove the times grow worse and worse.

Some of Mather's songs were extremely coarse, especially when they were about some magistrate, clergyman or employer who was disliked by the poorer Sheffield folk.

For example, when Mr. Watkinson, who was Master Cutler in 1787, demanded the supply of thirteen knives to the dozen, the trade found vent for their indignation through a ballad by Mather, which had the following verse:

'Then may the odd knife his great carcase dissect,
Lay open his vitals for men to inspect,
A heart full of black as the infernal gulf,
In that greedy, bloodsucking, bonescraping wolf!'

An example of the conditions existing in Sheffield town during Mather's lifetime are expressed in the following poem:

'Where slowly down the vale a river runs,
Of dark complexion like its crooked sons;
In a fair country, stands a filthy town,
By bugs and butchers held in high renown;
Sheffield the Black—in ugliness supreme;
Yet ugly Sheffield is my dirty theme.'

The poet then goes on to mention the unlovely buildings and the volume of smoke which rises from the town, until the sun 'hangs like a copper shield'. Then when it rains, the writer tells us:

'Ah, luckless he, who in unhappy hour
Is doomed to walk our streets beneath the shower,
No friendly spout from the projecting eaves,
The copious tribute of the clouds receives,
But headlong from the roof, in sooty showers,
Prone on the hapless passenger it pours.
While on our moonless evenings, dark and damp,
Imprudent thrift denies the public lamp
And many a dunghill graces many a street.'

The poet then refers to the streets of Sheffield after very heavy rain and continues:

'Whole streams of rubbish and whole seas of mud;
With turnip tops, potato peelings join,
And to their cast garments, peas and beans combine,
Providing pigs and ducks with goodly cheer;
To pigs and ducks our streets are ever dear,
May no audacious scavenger presume to wield the rake, the shovel or the broom!'

Customs and conditions in Old Sheffield Town

An old custom of Sheffield long since passed into obscurity, was the way of showing respect for the dead by the sending of 'Berring' or burying cakes to the relatives of the deceased. The Berring Cakes were wrapped in white writing paper and sealed with black sealing wax. The larger the size of the cake the greater the respect shown or so it was assumed.

Joseph Mather wrote a song called 'Round Legs' and part of one verse was:

'Round Legs to Wadsley went,
With berring cakes he was sent,'
etc.

Round Legs was the nickname of the man who worked as carrier for a baker's shop.

Legislation against the workers during the 18th century was extremely severe.

If a workman refused to work the hours offered, at the rate offered, he was fined £10, and if he couldn't pay which was usually the case, he got twenty days imprisonment on bread and water. For a second offence the fine was doubled and if he could not pay he was fastened in the pillory. For a third offence the fine was £40 and in default he was put in the pillory and had one of his ears cut off!

One can appreciate why, when in 1727 advertisements appeared offering great advantages to filesmiths if they would settle in France, the workmen of Sheffield began to dispose of their effects and to pack up their tools for the journey. This so worried Judge Jessop of Broom Hall that he petitioned the King, asking him to prevent the departure of the workmen. The King granted the petition.

However, in 1732 a Filesmiths' Benefit Society was established and this was quickly followed by the Cutler's Carpenters', Grinders', Masons', Braziers' and other societies. These were the forerunners of the now powerful trade unions.

The Wesleyan Methodists met with much opposition when they founded their first chapels in Sheffield. In 1743 the little chapel they had built in Pinstone Lane was completely demolished by rioters.

Through the whole of the winter of 1766, Mulberry Street Chapel was repeatedly attacked by ruffians and foul names were hurled at the people entering the building. Women in particular bore the brunt of these attacks and their cloaks and gowns were often slashed with knives.

A favourite trick of the ruffians would be to enter the chapel with a cat or fowl tucked underneath their coats. These would then make loud noises during the service, annoying the preacher and the congregation alike.

At one time the objectors to the Methodists climbed up the outside of the chapel to the skylight, which was situated just over the pulpit. There they made such a nuisance of themselves by mimicking the preacher that shutters had to be fixed over the window. After this the rioters threw stones at the locked doors and battered on them with wooden clubs.

The greatest evil in those times was drunkenness and this was not confined just to the poorer classes. Outside many of the public houses were signs reading, 'Get drunk for a penny, dead drunk for twopence and have clean straw for nothing'.

The hours of work for most people were extremely long and in 1759 tailors would work from six o'clock in the morning to eight o'clock in the evening for a princely wage of three shillings (15 pence).

Most of the cutlers' premises were very small, with a shop at the front and a forge in the yard behind. The shop would be entered by a low doorway and down a stone step. Written orders for the chapman who came round and distributed his favours according to the samples shown, were stuck in the leaden casement of the windows and thereafter formed a subject of comment for the people passing by. The workmen were frequently bandy legged owing to the cramped position in which they worked.

Street conditions were very bad at this time, most of the narrow lanes and alleys being dirty and badly lit. As one poet wrote:

'When dingy oil lamps shone at neet,
Like glow worms in a wood;
When we could scarcely pick betweet
The causeway from the mud.'

By the mid nineteenth century conditions for the working people of Sheffield had slightly improved. However, most folk were still poor and there were many beggars, who, more often than not, were women with children.

Very few people bought a newspaper, but would rely for their knowledge of what was going on in the world on the placards placed on the streets by the newspaper publishers.

When children were lost, the mother would chalk on the pavement, 'Lost a little boy of two years. Return to Mrs. so and so.' or words to that effect.

Poultry was kept in the cellars of many of the houses, the fowls being allowed to roam the streets during the daytime, to scratch for food amongst the rubbish thrown all around.

In the little house-shop windows many delicacies were for sale, including bundles of halfpenny treacle sticks, wrapped in brightly coloured paper. Home made butterscotch and forthcakes (treacle parkin) were also on sale. To delight young children there were sheep, cows and dogs made in pastry, with currants for eyes and lemon peel for mouths. It was a common sight to see boys and girls chewing liquorice root or eating the locust bean.

Entertainment in Old Sheffield

The entertainment of Sheffield folk in olden times was often of a violent and brutal nature. Cock fighting was common up to 1830, when the last (official) cock fight took place on the Manor. The same year also saw the last badger baiting in the Hyde Park area. Bull baiting was also a favourite pastime, a bull being firmly chained to a stake fixed in the ground, whilst savage dogs were allowed to attack it. Bull baiting took place in the Haymarket, which was originally called 'Bullstake'. On the Moor rat worrying was a common practice, the contest being to see how many rats could be worried by terriers in a given time.

The 'well to do' indulged in fox hunting and there is an amusing story of a hunt that took place in 1804.

It appears that the huntsmen and hounds of Sir William Chambers Bagshawe, of the Oakes in Norton, after a long chase had followed the fox into the village of Attercliffe. The fox took refuge in a public house, but the hounds failed to find it and after a time the huntsmen called the dogs off. The following morning it was found that the fox had taken refuge in a large sett pot in the kitchen and as soon as the public house door was opened the fox shot out and was away!

Feasts, or fairs, were the highlight of the year for the working class people and in the 'Shevvild Chap's Song Book' one of these is aptly described in verse:

'A few months since on frolic bent,
On a journey to Little Sheffield Feast I went,
And being as all of your know quite green,
I was mortally pleased with the sights I'd seen:
There was Betty and Jenny and Factory Nan,
And twenty more girls and they each had a man,
And Sally and Sukey, and Bandy-leg'd Jack,
And the chap that sold pies with his can on his back,
There were donkeys and dog-carts, and lots of fine folks,
With their jaws all a cracking their nuts and their jokes,
As hungry as hunters from biggest to least,
All right for a blow out at Little Sheffield Feast.'

Football in those days was not quite the same as today. For instance, in 1854 a match took place at Bents Green between Norton and Sheffield. The colours of the Norton men were red, while the Sheffielders wore green.

Before the match began it was noticed that the Sheffield supporters had turned up in such force that it was advisable for the Norton team to send for reinforcements and this they did. As usual after the match a general battle commenced and many of the Sheffield men, who in those days wore their hair very long and tied in a 'tail', lost this part of their anatomy.

The result of this match and the ensuing fight caused quite a stir and for some days afterwards no Norton man dared show his face in Sheffield town.

Naturally the public houses were the favourite venue of most of the folk and there were very many of these establishments, both large and small, in the town.

Some of the most well known were also coaching inns, and amongst these were the Angel, the Tontine and the King's Head. Of the four ancient public houses that existed in High Street: The Grey Horse, The White Bear, The Bay Childers and The Blue Bell, only the last named remains today and that in name only.

A public house situated in Waingate was called the Rose and Crown. Built in 1813 it was so renowned for its beer, that the following poem was composed in honour of the beverage:

'The Rose and Crown
In Sheffield town,
The landlord's name George Hartley,
He brews good ale,
It is not stale,
Where 'tis I'll tell you shortly.
It's in Waingate,

Which is not straight,
And leads into the Wicker,
Call as you pass,
And take a glass,
'Twill make you travel quicker!'

In the eighteenth and nineteenth centuries many theatres were opened in Sheffield, though theatrical shows were given before that time in a building situated through the yard of the Angel Inn in Angel Street.

One of the early theatres was the Surrey Music Hall, West Bar, one of the first of its kind in the United Kingdom, certainly the most beautiful, and second only to Covent Garden in London. It had a splendid ballroom surrounded by enormous mirrors and magnificent pictures. Unfortunately fire broke out on 25th March, 1865, and the whole building was gutted. The ruins of this fine theatre remained until 1880, when they were cleared away to permit the building of the Union Offices.

There was also the Alexandra Theatre, usually called the 'Old Alex', which closed in 1914, and the Alhambra, destroyed by fire in 1882. Others, within recent memory, were the Hippodrome, the Theatre Royal, the Albert Hall, the Empire and the Lyceum. The last named, though still in existence, is not in use, though the auditorium is 'listed' as being of historic and architectural interest.

In 1838 Johann Strauss, the elder, visited Sheffield, and an advertisement in the Sheffield Mercury of 6th October stated:

'THEATRE ROYAL, SHEFFIELD.

The celebrated Valze Composer from Vienna, with his unrivalled orchestra composed of 28 artistes, begs respectfully to announce a Grand Evenings Concert to take place on Thursday, October, 11th, 1838, on which occasion he will introduce a selection of his compositions as performed by him at the Courts of Austria, Prussia, France, Holland, Belgium and at the Coronation in London.

Prices of admission — 5/-, 2/6d and 1/6d.'

Whether these were special prices is not stated, but it is interesting to note that the following week admission was 3/-, 2/- and 1/-.

During the summertime a favourite resort, especially of the young ladies was the Botanical Gardens. The Gardens were opened in 1836 and occupied eighteen acres of land between Clarkehouse Road and Ecclesall Road. In the good weather 'promenades' were held, when the ladies, dressed in their finery, promenaded, chatted and flirted to the music of a band. It was always said at the time that 'though marriages may be made in heaven, many Sheffield marriages were hatched at the Proms!'

Galas were often held in the Botanical Gardens and all kinds of amusements were staged. On one occasion, Blondin, the world famous tight rope walker, performed his daring feats above the tree tops. As the prices of admission to these galas were very low, it was not unusual to have crowds of twenty to thirty thousand people listening to the music and enjoying the entertainment.

Today the Gardens are under the care of the Sheffield Parks Department, and provide an oasis of colour, peace and pleasure, in between the surrounding busy roads.

The odd characters of Sheffield

> 'Mary Ann of Sheffield is my name,
> England is my nation,
> Sheffield is my place of birth,
> And Sheffield my limitation!'

Sheffield of the nineteenth and early twentieth centuries had many famous and odd characters who were well known to all and sundry, usually by their first names or nickname.

There was, for example, 'Uppsy Daisy', who used to play a concertina in Norfolk Park. It is said this man got his nickname for the time when he saw a small boy fall down in front of a fast moving horse and trap. Running into the road he pulled the child from under the horse's hooves, dusted the boy down and said simply, 'Uppsy Daisy!'

A man who sold laces and bits of leather for repairing boots, was called 'Tacking Ends', and a coloured man, well known in the East End, was always known as 'Snowball'.

Doctor Durrant

Doctor Durrant was always driven through the streets of Sheffield by a coachman dressed in fine livery. Every few minutes, as they travelled along, the coachman would blow upon a long horn, with the good doctor bawling out, 'Blow, Joe, blow!' intermixed with other expletives I dare not mention.

The doctor was very fond of drink and would patronise most of the public houses which were situated on his 'rounds'. Good naturedly he would ask his coachman what he would have to drink? The wily coachman, who did not believe in drinking ale if he could have something stronger, would always reply, 'Same as you, Mester, same as you!'

The Blind Fiddlers

Many blind fiddlers existed in Sheffield in the nineteenth century and the 'Q in the Corner', a public house in Paradise Square, was a well known resort for these entertainers.

The landlord of the 'Q in the Corner', Samuel Goodlad, had a very fine memory for music, and he claimed the right to play the first fiddle on all public occasions. He would boast he had all the new tunes from London and played them before any other person.

On one occasion Samuel performed a new tune for the benefit of his customers, but was unaware that some men had carried into the public house, hidden inside a sack, a blind fiddler called Stephen.

While Samuel was being congratulated on his playing, the sack was carried out again and Blind Stephen released.

He then re-entered the public house to be met by his conspiritors who called to him, asking him if he could play the tune that Samuel Goodlad said only he knew! Blind Stephen said, 'Of course I can, and better than anyone else in the town!' Whereupon the aggrieved landlord bet him 'a leg of mutton and trimmings' if he could play the tune. The blind fiddler, having an even keener ear for music than Samuel, played the tune perfectly and won the wager!

When Stephen left the 'Q in the Corner', it was past midnight. He explained to the landlord's new wife, who didn't know that he was blind, that he was not afraid of seeing a ghost, but as it was a dark night, please could he borrow a lantern?

The kind hearted landlady said it was a favour she couldn't deny, so she told a servant girl to get one for him.

Equipped with his lantern the jovial fiddler set off towards Pinstone Lane, but he hadn't gone very far when someone asked the landlady why she had lent a lantern to a blind man? Thinking she would be a laughing stock if word got around, the landlady sent the servant girl after Blind Stephen to retrieve the lantern.

However, Blind Stephen refused to give it up. The girl argued with him, saying how useless a lantern was to a blind man, but Stephen just laughed and said, 'Does think I borrowed it for me sen? Tell thy mistress that there are so many drunken folk in the streets that if one knocked me down and smashed my fiddle I should be ruined. I am much obliged to her for the lantern and although I can't see it, others can!'

Blind John and his wife

Another story of these fiddlers concerns Blind John and his wife. These two were beggars and could always be seen in the neighbourhood of Saville Street and Attercliffe Road. They would beg for money and occasionally sing a hymn to the scrapings of John's fiddle.

On one occasion they had sung five or six verses of a hymn when John ceased playing and inquired of his wife, 'Is anybody about?' 'No, John, nob'dy!' was the reply. 'Come along then,' grumbled Blind John, 'We can sing Come to Jesus till hell fetches us, but if there's nob'dy about, nob'dy 'ill gi'e us owt!'

Charlie Milner

Charlie Milner had an ironmonger's shop in Fargate. He was a friendly character, but rather like our present politicians, he could never answer a question with a straight yes or no.

One day some grinders made a wager that a straight yes or no COULD be got from him. Accordingly two of them went to the ironmonger's shop and enquired, 'Mr. Milner, does a coach go from here to Baslow every day?'

However, the wager was lost, for Charlie instantly replied with a question, 'Does thou want to go to Baslow then?'

The Turkey Rhubarb Sellers

These characters used to stand amidst the tripe venders in King Street. They would keep up a constant barrage of chatter to the crowd, but their favourite spiel was always the same. 'Real Genuine turkey rhubarb . . . Mine Uncle goes to Turkey vonce every year and comes back twice a year. The real genuine turkey rhubarb!'

People would stand, listen, gaze and wonder, at the rhubarb sellers, meanwhile consuming penn'orths of tripe.

The Compulsive Gambler

William Lee, who lived in High Street in the 18th century, was a well known gambler and a very regular frequenter of the 'Bay Childers' public house.

Naturally Lee made a point of attending all the local races and one day, on his way to Doncaster, he noticed the coach in front swaying very violently.

This coach was carrying Lee's wife and only son, but his betting instinct being so strong, William shouted to his friend sitting beside him, 'Five to four that carriage turns over and our John is killed!'

Sequah

Sequah wasn't a Sheffield man, but he was a favourite character with the town's folk of the late 19th century.

He would come to Sheffield dressed as a cowboy and wearing a large stetson hat. Usually hiring the Drill Hall, he would drive there in a gilt carriage drawn by cream ponies, escorted by a large band of cowboys.

Sequah would then dress as an Indian chief whilst he extracted teeth, cured rheumatism and attended to many other complaints. The cries of the people having their teeth extracted were drowned by a terrific noise made by the cowboy band!

The real name of this showman dentist was Hannaway Rowe and when he retired he went to live in a small herbalist's shop in Southampton. He died in 1934 having reached the ripe old age of ninety-three.

How Grinder Jim received his Foot-ale

Before the advent of steam, most grinding work was carried on at the water wheels which abounded on all the rivers of Sheffield. In these workshops, or grinding hulls, it was an ancient custom that whenever a workman joined the wheel, got married or had a child, money must be given by him for ale to celebrate the occasion.

In a grinding hull on the River Sheaf one of the grinders was a young man called Jack Grindleblade, who was courting the pretty daughter of 'Buffing' Bill. The couple had decided to get married at Whitsuntide and when the big day arrived Jack and Molly went to the Parish Church in Sheffield, to come out later as man and wife. All Jack's workmates were waiting at the church door and the groom soon found himself uncomfortable with his 'neckhole' stuffed full of rice!

From the church the couple walked to the home of Molly's father, where a fine spread was waiting. As was usual, most of the men had too much to drink, including the bridegroom, and later, reeling home, he was telling everyone in earshot that 'hish—wife sh—finest—gurl in—Shevvel!'

Jack was to discover in due course that his observation was completely accurate.

When he returned to work after the festivities, he was immediately pestered for the price of 'Wedding Ale', in other words—ten shillings.

Now Jack being a sensible chap, realized that now he was married, he couldn't afford to throw an half sovereign away, so he decided he had better ask his missis. For even in the short time that they had been wed, Molly had become the Chancellor of the Exchequer in their home.

A day or two later the newly married wife came proudly to the wheel, bringing her husband's dinner in a small wicker basket. 'Is t'mester in?' she asks, referring to her husband. 'He's not abaht, lass', shouts one of the men, who was known as Grinder Jim. 'Then I'll wait a bit—aw've brought his dinner,' said Molly.

At this the grinders decided that here was an opportunity for a laugh at the newlywed's expense, so Grinder Jim retorted with a huge grin, 'Then if tha' waits here, thah'll have to pay thi foot-ale!'

Thereupon the grinders gathered round the frightened girl, demanding ten shillings to drink her health. But the little woman was braver than they thought and she refused to pay.

Molly then found herself being seized by the half dozen grinning workmen, who carried her like a baby to the drum board and plonked her down. Grinder Jim knelt down and clutched one of her feet. 'Take her boot off, Jim!' shouted the grinders, thoroughly enjoying the woman's discomforture.

Many horrible thoughts raced through Molly's head, as she felt the men fumbling with her boot. What are the men going to do? Do they intend to denude me of all my clothing—to disrobe me until I stand before them like a cutler's Lady Godiva? Never, I will die first! Oh, that my husband would come to my rescue!

Meanwhile Grinder Jim had seized her left ankle and his right hand clasped her boot heel. 'Will thah pay thi foot-ale?' he demanded savagely.

'No!' cried Molly, white with passion and struggling wildly, 'But here's mi foot-ale!' And striking out with her right leg, she sent her heel with sledge hammer force into the grinder's chest!

Backwards the big man went, rolling down the slanting floor like a human football. His fellow grinders were convulsed with glee, for the look of amazement on Grinder Jim's face was ludicrous to behold.

The chances are that if he had not been stopped by the door post, the man would have rolled down the bank into the River

Sheaf. As it was his mouth and eyes were rimmed with wheelswarf, his face was bruised, his head cut and his chest as sore as if a horse had kicked him.

When the men turned from viewing the 'mighty fallen', they were just in time to see Molly stalking indignantly out of the grinding wheel. But not until she had disappeared did Jim get up, to rub his bruises and to wipe the wheelswarf off his teeth. Then amidst the scoffing of his mates he went home, finally resolved that he would negotiate for 'foot-ale' no more.

Just a year afterwards Molly presented her husband with a bouncing baby boy, but Jack Grindleblade was never asked for 'child's-ale', the ten shillings that was normally levied on a grinder when his first child was born!

The Jolly Grinder

From a street ballad printed by Joseph Ford.

> 'There was a jolly grinder once,
> Liv'd by the River Don;
> He work'd and sang from morn to night,
> And sometimes he'd work none!
> But still the burden of his song,
> For ever used to be—
> Tis never worth while to work too long,
> For it doesn't agree with me!'

Mary Ann of Malin Bridge

During the time when water power was the main method of turning grinding wheels and working trip hammers, a local saying amongst the grinders and workers of the wheels on the River Loxley was, 'Mary Ann has been in her pattens!'

This saying originated because of the habit of the grinders, who, during the week, would go for ale to a public house at Malin Bridge, kept by a woman called Mary Ann. They would ask for the ale consumed to be 'put on the slate', giving their promise to pay in full at the weekend.

If any of the wheels defaulted, Ann would go in the night to that particular wheel and remove the drive band or belt that turned the grindstones. The wheel would not receive the drive band back until the previous week's debt had been paid.

Pattens were the wooden shoes or clogs worn at that time, hence the favourite saying when a drive belt was off or anyone's tools were missing, 'Mary Ann has been in her pattens!'

The strange story of Benjamin Garside Elliott

Most Sheffield people will have heard of Ebenezer Elliott, the poet who came to live in the town in 1821, made a fortune here, and because of his poems against the cruel 'Corn Laws', had a statue erected to his memory in the Market Place.

However, few will know of the following story of the strange end of the eccentric Benjamin Garside Elliott, one of Ebenezer's sons.

Benjamin lived practically all his life in a little hamlet north of Sheffield called Shiregreen. His cottage presented a poor picture, always in a state of disrepair, the windows broken, with shutters usually kept closed, and a weed grown, neglected garden.

The interior of the cottage was to most people a 'mysterious unknown'. Boys living in the village believed the place to be full of arms and weapons, a tale probably spread around after the milk boy had spotted a rusty gun when Benjamin had opened the door slightly to receive his milk.

Benjamin never let anyone enter his home and he seldom left it himself except for walks which he always took at the strange hour of midnight. Sometimes on these nocturnal ramblings he would meet the village policeman and they would walk along together. Because Benjamin always armed himself with a bill-hook and carried a pistol in his pocket, wild tales were circulated about him amongst the folk of Shiregreen and Wincobank.

However, in reality the man was harmless and he would probably have been as amazed as anybody at the tales told about him.

One Sunday, in December, 1867, he confided to his friend the policeman, that he had an apprehension of approaching death and that was the last time he was seen alive!

The following day, which had been preceded by a very cold night, the milk boy received no response to his knock, but because of Benjamin's eccentricity, he took no notice at the time.

However, when the recluse failed to open the door again on the Tuesday, the milk boy went for help and the cottage door was forced open.

On the floor of the kitchen, in wonderful confusion, lay clothes, food, domestic utensils, weapons, books, newspapers and piles of miscellaneous lumber! Then by the sinkstone they saw the body of Benjamin, lying where he had collapsed, obviously early on Monday morning.

Though the mystery of the cottage had now been revealed, the villagers still had their misgivings about this house of death and the little crowd waited outside the door for the arrival of the authorities from Sheffield.

Examination of the contents of the cottage revealed that Benjamin had been no ordinary recluse. Various books and writings proved that he had possessed considerable power of mind, and that he had had excellent taste in art was evinced by the fine paintings that adorned the walls and the quality and character of the furniture.

By the couch where he would recline and read, a well worn copy of Mrs. Shelley's 'Frankenstein' was found.

What a pity it seems, that the son of such a noted poet, should at his end become a gazing stock for the local rustics and that all that could be said at the time was compressed into the laconic verdict of the coroner's jury—'Found dead!'

The friendly ghost of Bramley Hall

Situated in Bramley Hall Road, Handsworth, is a fine building known as Bramley Hall. Though now surrounded by a housing estate, this hall is said to be haunted by a friendly ghost!

It appears that when the first hall on this site was occupied by Hugh de Bramley, a Norman lord, who lived in the 13th century; a monk coming from Kirkstead Abbey in Lincolnshire, to Sheffield, was attacked by thieves and left lying badly injured in a hedgerow not far from Bramley Hall.

The following day servants of De Bramley discovered this unfortunate holy man and upon their master's bequest, they carried him to Bramley Hall. There he was given a bed and his wounds attended to.

However, the poor fellow had been hit upon the head many times, causing deep wounds and a considerable loss of blood, and this, together with the lack of medical knowledge at the time, caused his death the following day.

An ancient legend says that each year, on the anniversary of that foul murder, the monk returns to Bramley Hall, to wander around the garden and rooms of the beautiful Georgian house that now occupies the site.

No one need be frightened of this ghost however, for, because of the kind treatment bestowed upon him by Hugh de Bramley and his staff, the phantom monk wears a benevolent smile and holds out his hands in benediction should he be seen by any mortal being.

The unfortunate John Unwin of Dore

In the early 19th century, there lived at Dore a man called John Unwin who, it seems, was a very keen inventor.

One of his inventions was a diving bell which was sent to Manchester to be tested and proved very satisfactory.

Unfortunately however, a workman in the Manchester factory, fascinated by the unusual machine, climbed inside when no one was about, and lowered the bell into about twelve feet of water. Not being familiar with the controls, he must have pressed some of the wrong buttons, for water rushed into the diving bell and he was instantly drowned.

This accident so enraged all the other workmen that they smashed the invention completely and they would also have done serious injury to John Unwin if they could have laid hands upon him.

This mishap ended, for ever, the Dore man's inventions in the diving world!

The story of Betty and the Whatcake

One wet Monday morning in the eighteen-hundred's, an old woman who lived just outside the village of Dore, passed down the village street. She was obviously dressed in her best clothes, with pattens on her feet and she proudly carried her one and only umbrella.

The village school mistress happened to be standing at the door of the school, which was also her cottage, and she was extremely surprised to see Betty at such an unusual time. So she called, 'Betty, where are you going?' 'I'm for the chapel', answered Betty, surprised at being questioned. 'Ah, going to be married?' asked the schoolmistress, with a broad smile. 'Noo!' was Betty's response. 'What then?' was the next question. 'What do we go every Sunday for?' Betty replied.

A look of amazement came over the school teacher's face. 'Sunday! but it's Monday today!' she exclaimed. 'The ferrits it is!' grumbled Betty, realization dawning, 'Then its the old whatcake (oatcake) what's done it!' 'But how's that?' asked the schoolmistress. 'Why', responded Betty, 'I always bake a peck of meal and it just serves me a week, but it happened to make two cakes more this time and that's driven me into Monday'.

'What makes it worse', continued the old woman, apparently horrified at breaking the Sabbath, 'I was white-washing yesterday!'

The pleasures of ballooning

In the late 19th century a favourite sport for the well-to-do adventurous person was ballooning. Many accounts are recorded of various ascents, but I think the following gives a perfect picture of the thrills and entertainment provided by the sport.

The balloon, which was the property of Spencers of London, was due to leave the Botanical Gardens just after one o'clock in the afternoon. The day was fine, with a clear sky and the wind seemed ideal for the ascent. Crowds of people had paid to enter the gardens to witness the daring aeronauts set forth on their journey.

A local man, Mr. E. Parker Hydes, of Nether Edge, was the chief aeronaut and at one forty p.m. he decided that conditions were right for the take off. Upon his shout, the rope holders let go and the balloon started to drift away in a south westerly direction. It then appeared that there was the possibility of a nasty accident, as some large poplar trees stood directly in the path of the rising balloon. Luckily a slight variation in the wind saved the aeronauts from disaster.

As the crowd cheered lustily, the balloon rose steadily and, as Mr. Hydes remarked later, 'What a pity that Sheffield should be enveloped in so much smoke, otherwise as we hung between Ranmoor and Ecclesall, we should have seen it from end to end!'

Though only in the air for ten minutes, the balloon had reached a height of 2,000 feet and people watching in Nether Edge, Heeley and Meersbrook, had an excellent view of the ascent.

The daring aeronauts then passed over Dore Station, leaving Ecclesall on the right. Now the balloon was at an height of 3,000 feet and passing over Totley, with miles of beautiful moorland country on the left and ahead. This made a glorious panorama, with Holmsfield Church and the Owler Bar Inn as easily recognisable features.

Keeping to the same height, the balloon passed over Chatsworth, the River Derwent and Rowsley.

As with most balloon flights, the landing was the most dangerous, but luckily a good set down was made in a field near Hoon, about one mile from Tutbury Station. The aeronauts then walked across the fields to a farmhouse, where the farmer agreed to lend a horse and cart to carry the collapsed balloon away.

The daring travellers then caught the six o'clock train to Derby Station, where they had refreshments. Afterwards they left Derby on the 8 o'clock train and they returned to Sheffield after what they described as 'a most enjoyable day!'

An advertisement later inserted in the 'Weekly Independent' of 1894, stated: 'Anyone wanting to take a trip and view the wonders of nature, should contact Mr. E. Parker Hydes, of Nether Edge, who will gladly arrange for an ascent upon a favourable day.'

An early Aeronautical Engineer

One does not usually connect Sheffield with the invention of the aeroplane, but it is an interesting fact that one of Sheffield's sons had a no mean part to play in the study of engine powered flight!

This happened when John Stringfellow, who was born at Attercliffe on 6th December, 1799, designed and constructed the first ever engine driven model aeroplane to make a free flight.

John's father had also had a great interest in science and mechanics and he encouraged his son in his studies.

The engines made for the model planes were steam driven and had the highest power/weight ratio of that time.

John Stringfellow died on 13th December, 1883, aged 84 years.

Double 'uns in Paradise Square

Without a doubt one of the most fascinating places in Sheffield is Paradise Square, a fine cobbled open space surrounded by houses built in 1736 and 1771.

Originally a cornfield, it was leased in 1736 by Thomas Broadbent, who lived in the 'Old Banker's House', still standing in Hartshead. It was he who built most of the houses we see today.

An old poem gives an insight into the Paradise Square of ancient days:

'You may form to your fancy a stile which once stood
Near the little Grape Tavern and made up of wood;
On the side of a field then belonging to Hicks,
Where children at that time hav't oft gathered sticks,
'Twas called "Hicks Stile Field" and there corn was oft grown,
But "Paradise Row" since the stile was took down,
Many years it continued with houses, one row,
But now 'tis a beautiful square as you know,
With a Freemasons' Lodge and a flight of stone stairs,
And under it shops with various wares.'

One house in Paradise Square had a cellar kitchen where griddle cakes, oat cakes, pikelets, etc., were made.

A flight of steps leading to this kitchen had a half door at the top. A lady who was a caretaker at the house, getting old, engaged a 'strapping wench' from the country, to assist her with her work.

As to be expected, within weeks a local lad came a-courting and this was mostly carried on over the half door at the top of the steps.

One day the old lady remarked to a neighbour that she thought there would soon be a wedding judging by the kissing she heard.

She then added, 'I counted up to twenty, but when "double 'uns" started I lost count!'

How Heeley Duff'em acquired its name

The ancient village of Heeley even today is often referred to by the local folk as 'Heeley Duff'em', although few people know how the nickname originated.

In olden times the little stream called the Meers Brook was the boundary between Yorkshire and Derbyshire. The path of the stream is through Meersbrook under the main Chesterfield Road (just above Albert Road) at Heeley, from where it flows into the River Sheaf at Saxon Bridge. Immediately over the culvert that carries the stream under Chesterfield Road, was the Heeley Toll Bar, a situation that meant when the toll gate was closed it was in Yorkshire, but when it was opened it was in Derbyshire. This led to the proud boast by the toll keeper that he had walked from Yorkshire into Derbyshire and back more times than any other man!

In the old days people were often sent to prison for debt, for very few working class people had any possessions worth selling. As the Sheffield bailiffs had no jurisdiction in Derbyshire, a person could escape being sent to jail by simply crossing over the Meers Brook at Heeley.

As the area near the toll bar was the nearest into Derbyshire, it was generally assumed that folk going to live at Heeley were going there to 'duff' (i.e. not pay) their creditors.

Later when the County Court Acts were passed giving Sheffield jurisdiction right into Derbyshire as far as Norton and Greenhill, it was then of no advantage to live at Heeley, but the nickname has stuck!

The Nosey Ecclesfield Folk

Letters to the editors of local newspapers often give an amusing and illuminating insight into the manners of the times and the following extract, from a letter to the 'Weekly Independent' of 1875, amply illustrates this point.

'From Southey the passerby has a fine view of Walkley, than which there is no more creditable suburb of Sheffield. These odd cottages in their little garden plots speak volumes for the industry and thrift of the cutlers and grinders by whom they were mainly built.

The district north of Wadsley Bridge, of which Ecclesfield is the centre, is peopled by, I grant, a good hearted, but most bad mannered race of people. Every woman at her doorstead, every group at the street corner, every straggler in the street make the stranger the centre of a stolid stare. Hereabouts everybody knows everybody else and their business, and the countenances of everybody seem to denote that the thoughts within are, 'Who's that?', 'Where's he going?', 'What's he doing?' and so forth!'

A remarkable suite of furniture

Sheffield craftsmen have made many beautiful and exquisite works of art over the last three hundred years, but nothing can have been more remarkable than the suite of furniture made for an Indian Rajah, in 1904, by the firm of Mappin and Webb.

The furniture, constructed mostly of solid silver, comprised: a four poster bed, twelve dining room and easy chairs, two couches, four tables, a drawing room cabinet and a lady's dressing table.

The bedstead was eight feet long by six feet broad and thirteen feet six inches high. On it were beautiful panels depicting in relief allegorical representations of Sleep, after pictures painted by Albert Moore, R.A.

All the furniture was in Chippendale and French marquetry style. Light frames of oak were made for the chairs, upon which sterling silver was solidly fitted, with upholstery of rich Indian Silk brocade. The tables were entirely of solid silver!

One can only guess at the cost of this wonderful silver suite, as the price paid was never divulged. Obviously the cost would be astronomical, even allowing for the lower prices existing at that time.

A Willow tree from Napoleon's Tomb

Just off the main Barnsley Road, at its junction with Norwood Road, lies the once sleepy little hamlet of Crabtree. Here can still be seen 'Rose Cottage', a delightful house built in the late seventeenth century.

In the garden of Rose Cottage is a tree of unusual ancestry.

It appears that this willow tree was planted in the early nineteen-twenties by Mrs. Franklin, whose husband owned the cottage and who was manager of Handbridges of Fargate.

Mrs. Franklin, before marriage, had been for many years a companion to a wealthy family who travelled around the world a great deal, and a member of this family took a cutting from the willow tree that grows on Napoleon's tomb at St. Helena.

When Mrs. Franklin married, she took a cutting from this tree and planted it in her garden. Later when she came to live at Rose Cottage, Mrs. Franklin took a cutting from the third tree and this has now grown and flourishes at Crabtree.

The Bellman, The Lamplighter, The Baker and The Sweep

In the early nineteenth century advertising was done by the official bellman, a fellow named Ward, who lived in Milk Street.

Old Ward as he was always called, had a smart uniform comprising of a blue coat, with red facings and bright buttons and he wore a tall hat with a broad gold band. He carried a large brass bell which he would ring loudly to attract attention. He then 'cried' the advertisements, gave notice of public meetings, auctions, etc., and also informed of lost children or articles.

Street lighting when gas lamps were first introduced was a rather primitive affair and necessitated a man carrying a ladder which he had to climb at each lamp post, so that he could light the gas with a match or small hand lamp.

The carrying of the ladders round some of the narrow streets of Sheffield caused quite a few incidents, such as the one that happened at the Norfolk Street end of George Street.

Turning the sharp corner, a lamplighter called Jim Elliott, inadvertently poked his ladder into the stomach of a man coming along George Street. At the same time as he swung the ladder round Jim called out 'Mind!'

The poor chap who had suffered the blow, asked ruefully, 'Why, Ar ta goin' to do it ageen?'

Many antiquated methods were used by Sheffield tradesmen of those times, one of these being very evident at the bakehouse of 'Baker George', which existed next to the Old Barleycorn, a public house in Coal Pitt Lane.

George had a long wooden trough fitted to the floor and in this he kneaded the dough by treading it in the same way as men used to tread clay for making steel melting pots.

With his trousers rolled up to his knees, the baker trod the dough with his bare feet and everyone acknowledged that without doubt Baker George produced the best bread in Sheffield!

Ted Mills was born in the vicinity of Broomhall Street in 1839 and at the age of eight years was apprenticed to a chimney sweep.

In those days the method of cleaning a chimney was to send young boys equipped with a small brush up the chimney to dislodge the soot. This was collected in sacks for later sale to local farmers.

Ted had to climb the chimneys stark naked, working all day, and for this he received the magnificent wage of two pence a week. His employer was very hard, 'a bad man an' all 'e wor', Ted remarked later in life.

As the sweep's wife kept a small shop, one condition of Ted's employment was that he spent all his two pence there.

The boy was only once stuck in a chimney, but he was fast for two hours and it was rather frightening. However, at one time he went up a public house chimney to rescue another sweep boy who was stuck and afterwards the grateful landlady gave Ted six pence and a bottle of ginger beer. The young chimney sweep never felt so rich as he did on that day!

Ted often had to sweep the chimneys at the town Hall, one of these chimneys having ten bends, making the cleaning a very difficult operation. One boy would work his way slowly to the top and he would send down the soot for another to catch in a sack. Sometimes Ted would sweep as many as thirty chimneys in a day.

Ted Mills carried on the trade all his life, until he died in 1921 at the age of eighty-two. Neither he or his wife could read or write, but both had great powers of mental arithmetic when it came to reckoning up the bills!

Dooleyism on The Victoria Railway Station

The old London and North Eastern Railway Station, at the end of the Wicker, is a maze of tunnels, lifts and bridges and these were put to a singular use in the nineteen-twenties by a porter named Dooley.

At that time the porter's wages were very low and these men relied upon tips to make a reasonable living. So that these tips were always forthcoming, Dooley would approach any hesitant travellers standing on one of the platforms and enquire which train they required. Upon being told it was the so and so train, Dooley would inform the passengers that they were on the wrong platform and picking up their luggage he would make the polite request, 'Follow me please'.

The wily porter would then take them along the platform, down a lift, through a tunnel under the line, up some steps, along a platform, over a bridge and after a few minutes of puffing and walking, would deposit the travellers and their luggage on some other part of the platform from which they had originally started.

Naturally the travellers would be greatly obliged to the helpful porter and a sixpenny tip would invariably be his reward.

This method of increasing their wages became very popular with some of the other porters at the old Victoria Station and the custom became known after its founder as 'Dooleyism'.

Some Quaint Customs of Ancient Days

A great event in Sheffield which survived right down to the year 1826 was the 'Summer Game'. It was not only a great attraction for the people, with its sports and games, but it was very profitable, especially in the year 1550.

At that time money was raised by the prodigious drinking of beer, brewed in the church house and sold at a high price. This was the chief means of supporting three chaplains of the Parish Church.

In early times a lot of importance was attached to the twelve days of Christmas. People would watch the sky during the whole of the twelve days, because they believed that as the weather was each day, so would be the weather of each month of the new year. The watchers would take it in turns to sit up at night and on the last day they each had a large share of a great plum cake.

In 1609 the Court Leet of Sheffield made a rule that nobody could walk or talk in the street from 9 o'clock in the evening till 3 o'clock in the morning, so as to annoy honest men and householders. Anyone breaking this rule was fined ten shillings. The curfew bell rang at 9 p.m. when everyone went to bed and the day bell rang at 4 a.m. the time for getting up and commencing work!

By another rule of the Court Leet, it was ordered that no person should make any wedding dinner for which he should take above sixpence a person and the penalty for so doing was £1 for each offence.

It was the custom in those days for the bridegroom to take the bride to his house immediately after the wedding and give a series of feasts extending over ten days or a fortnight. At these feasts the guests had to pay and the charge was such as to yield a considerable profit for the newly married pair and this money often set them up for a number of years.

The Legend of Ringinglow

On a certain Tuesday evening in the winter of a year in the eighteenth century, a Sheffield man lost his way when crossing the moors. The poor man tried for a long time to regain the path, but eventually he gave up in despair.

Suddenly he heard, very faintly in the distance, the sound of the bells of Sheffield Parish Church and following the direction of the sound, the traveller at last arrived safely home.

Feeling that the ringers of the bells had in all probability been the means of saving him from perishing on the bleak moors, he gave a sum of money to be divided among the ringers on that same night every year.

Because the Parish Church bells had been heard 'ringing low', from that time onwards that particular stretch of moorland was given the name it bears today.

Murder at Ringinglow

In April, 1876, quite a stir was created by an hoax concocted by a couple of rival journalists.

The first journalist, to boost sales of his newspaper, put out a placard in town which read, 'Horrid Murder in Ringinglow'. Not to be outdone a rival issued a similar placard bearing the legend, 'Body Found!'

These announcements caused scores of people to walk to Ringinglow to see what they could and naturally, after wandering about for hours and finding no trace of the murder, they finished up at the Norfolk Arms.

The landlord of that establishment was called Garrett and he did a roaring trade out of the weary travellers.

Were the journalists and the landlord in league? If so, it never came to light!

The Exhausted Cricketers

In the early nineteenth century the top of Carver Street was the limit of Sheffield in that direction. Where Carver Street Chapel now stands was a large piece of ground called Hutton Field.

This field was the principal cricket ground for the neighbourhood and many excellent matches were played there.

At one of these matches there was a player called Orsgethorpe who proved without doubt to be the best batsman of the day. When in, he either hit or blocked every ball and though the bowlers tried every way to get him out right through the whole day, they were unsuccessful. Eventually they were so tired they all lay down on the field in despair!

Needless to say Orsgethorpe's side won the match.

The Giant Pioneer

Past the top of Carver Street all was open country to the westward. At Trippet Lane the Grapes Public House was the end of Sheffield in that direction. Where Portobello Street now is, there was a long narrow lane, more like a gutter, with a high hedge on each side. Broad Lane finished at about what was to become the site of St. George's churchyard and all were fields and gardens beyond, except for here and there a gentleman's house.

Near the top of Trippet Lane lived a man called Curtis. He was very tall, being six feet two inches in height, was well built and very erect.

Naturally he entered the army as a volunteer in the Old Sheffield Blues, at the latter end of the seventeen-hundreds. When the commander saw the new recruit he was struck by his size and bearing and so he was immediately made a pioneer. He was then issued with a tall grenadier headdress that made him seem seven feet high and he was given a large hatchet to carry.

When on parade through the streets of Sheffield, Curtis led the regiment, looking, as one can imagine, a very formidable sight!

Post Office Cows

About this time the Post Office was in Orchard Street and mail coach drivers and the inhabitants complained about the office being in such a narrow street, with so many sharp corners.

The excuse made by the Postmaster for wanting that particular site was that he was able to keep his cows in the fields at the rear of his premises.

However, his successor, abiding by the wishes of the town people, opened a new post office at the corner of Arundel Street and Norfolk Street.

Climbing the Church Spire

The repair of church steeples in those days was carried out by a journeyman builder who used the method of nailing ladders against the side of the steeple, which was quicker and cheaper than ordinary scaffolding.

This builder was engaged to repair the Sheffield Parish Church spire and he commenced by nailing ladders right to the top of the steeple, so that he could then do the repair work with ease.

While this work was going on, William Batty came on the scene. Everyone in Sheffield knew that Batty never refused a dare, so he was challenged to climb to the top of the spire.

Batty not only climbed the steeple, but when at the top he played a tune on a French horn, much to the great amusement of the crowd watching below.

When Time Stood Still

Reliance in ancient days on the chiming of the Parish Church clock for telling the time, once saved a woman from spending a most uncomfortable night.

Martha Wright was a singer at the church and on this particular occasion, the sermon being rather dull, she had fallen asleep in one of the rear pews. When she awoke she found everyone had gone and that she was locked in the church.

She tried in vain to make herself heard, then suddenly had an idea. Going into the clock tower, she arrested the swing of the large pendulum, thereby stopping the clock and the chimes.

The absence of the usual indications of the passing of time attracted the attention of people around and upon investigation the woman was released.

The Legend of the Executioner

About the year 1700, a venerable old man, called William Walker, came to reside in the village of Darnall.

Walker turned out to be a man of wisdom, spending most of his time with books. He must also have had leanings towards astronomy for he was fond of gazing into the night sky, an occupation that caused some suspicion among the local people. This was also augmented by lack of communication, for Walker kept himself very much to himself and refused to be drawn into lenghty conversation.

Such a man—human nature being what it is—was soon the object of dislike by the rustic population. The story then spread around that William Walker was the same Walker who had cut off the head of King Charles I and that fearing for his safety after the Restoration, he had fled from the Court, to wander about the land until he eventually settled at Darnall.

Once this rumour was started nothing could stop it and even after the Cutlers' Company bestowed upon him the honorary freedom of their association, this never prevented the local people pointing out William Walker as the 'dreaded executioner'.

The Old Sheffield Volunteers

To be in the volunteers a working man had to sacrifice a great deal, for he lost a week's wages when in camp. The Hallamshire headquarters was situated in Eyre Street. The men drilled in civilian clothes and made a brave show marching down Matilda Street with the band in front.

The Artillery volunteers had their headquarters in Tudor Street, where the Lyceum Theatre is today. These men were very proud of their small round pill box hats.

The Yeomanry had both large and small horses and the men wore an helmet of similar style to the Life Guards. Their headquarters was in Norfolk Street.

Some of the horses used by the Yeomanry were used for drawing milk carts during the week. When parading through the town some wag would shout 'Milk!' and all the milk horses would stop dead, throwing the ranks into utter confusion!

Agony Column

The study of nineteenth century newspapers produces much that is enlightening and amusing, as, for example, this advertisement published in the Sheffield Mercury of April, 1833.

'An advertisement appeared a few days ago concerning a young lady who had eloped. She is most earnestly requested to return to her disconsolate parents; but, if she will not return, she is earnestly desired to send the key to the tea chest.'

There is no record of the result of this heartrending appeal!

Gallant Captain Bess

'Captain Bess' was the title given by the folk in the Sheffield area, to Elizabeth Birley of Middlewood House, who married William Longsdon, a member of an old Derbyshire family.

It appears that during a skirmish near Sheffield in the Civil War, Captain Longdon was seriously wounded. As often happened in those days, his wife, who was large with child, was among the spectators watching the battle. Being on horseback, Elizabeth, at great danger to herself, rode into the fray and rescued her husband. Leaving him with some friends, the gallant lady then returned to the field of battle and assumed command of her husband's men. Her wonderful bravery on this day earned her the title of 'Captain Bess'.

After the battle Elizabeth had her husband carried to Middlewood House, where, despite her tender care, he died of his wounds. Captain Longsdon was buried under the east window of the Sheffield Parish Church and within a few days of this sad event, 'Captain Bess' gave birth to a son.

A Legend of Loxley Common

It was a bitterly cold day in the year 1812, the sun had set early and low storm clouds hung over Loxley Common.

In a lonely cottage on the bleak moorland, a mother crooned over her sleeping baby, meanwhile listening for the sound of her husband's footsteps. Lomas Revill, gamekeeper to the lord of the Manor, was late and for his wife it was a weary vigil, relieved only by the visit of a woman friend from one of the cottages on the hillside.

When she had gone Mary Revill watched the flickering uncanny shadows cast by the log fire, until eventually, weariness overtaking her, she nodded off to sleep.

Struggling fitfully the moon sought to pierce the heavy snow clouds, but with little success and the wind howled across the common. As the hours passed the storm mounted in intensity and blinding snow swept the landscape until it was shrouded in a thick mantle of white.

The following day was New Year's Eve, and as morning broke, cold but fine, an acquaintance from the adjacent hamlet of Wadsley called to exchange the compliments of the day with the dwellers in the lonely cottage.

The visitor knocked again and again, but getting no response she tried the latch and finding the door would open, she entered the room.

A horrible sight met her eyes! Poor Mary Revill lay on the floor in a pool of blood—murdered! Whilst in the cradle near the body the baby lay fast asleep.

Outside the cottage the world was clad in white. During the night the snow had drifted all along the heath and piled itself upon the crags which formed a rough boundary between Loxley Common and Wadsley Common.

Leading from the cottage and right across the ridge and over the open common were large footprints, some partly obliterated by the drifting snow, but all leading in one direction, to a cave-like well, on the crown of the hill overlooking the valley. The footprints went distinctly to the cave, into it and disappeared.

Strangest of all, as far as could be discerned, there were no footprints leading out of the cave.

When the news of this terrible crime spread around the neighbouring hamlets, there was much weird speculation. Who was the murderer? What was the mystery of the footprints to the cave?

Meanwhile Lomas Revill had been found in the gamekeeper's cabin far out in the woods. When told of the tragic death of his wife he accepted the news with little show of surprise or emotion. Though he had been seen in the village inn, much the worse for drink, on the night of the tragedy, no one could swear that the gamekeeper hadn't spent the night in his cabin.

The moorland murder remained a mystery indeed and for years the good folk of the area fought shy of being anywhere near the Loxley cave after night had fallen.

As time went by, Lomas Revill became a strange man, prematurely aged with white hair, even though he was only 42 years old.

Another New Year's Eve came and once more the common was deep in snow. At the local inn someone remarked that he hadn't seen the gamekeeper for a number of days, so deciding to investigate, a number of men made up a party and went along to the cabin in the woods.

No trace being found of Lomas, they then tramped over the common to the old cottage, and there, in an outbuilding, they found his body—hanging from a rafter!

Later a search of the cabin in the woods revealed a hunter's knife, rusted in gore, and a pair of blood stained gaiters. Folk who had known Lomas Revill well said that he had always acted strangely when New Year's Eve came round and that he had often been heard to mutter that he couldn't stand life any longer.

Beyond this, and the articles found in the cabin, there was nothing to connect the gamekeeper with the murder of his wife.

However superstition had seized the simple, homely people of the countryside and when storm clouds frowned, when snow whistled in the wind over the common, and pale moonlight cast its haunting shadows on crag and heath, 'tis said the ghost of Mary Revill walked abroad.

Wanderers over the common and the lanes about, thought of Frank Fern's gibbet, creaking in the wind on the Edge only a stone's throw away and all but the stout hearted feared to pass that way at night lest they should hear the clanking of Frank Fern's chains or encounter the ghost of that poor unfortunate mother.

For many years afterwards a number of cottages stood empty, falling into ruin, because of the common's association with the murder of Mary Revill.

A walk from Sheffield to Beauchief in the Early Nineteenth Century

Based on fact and written in the style of that period

It was about noon on a delightful September day, when we departed from the King's Head in Change Alley, to walk to Beauchief.

My companions, Mr. and Mrs. Williams, relatives of my late dear wife, were in the course of spending a few days in Sheffield and I had promised to escort them, during their short stay, to see some of the country-side which is adjacent to our small town.

After bidding farewell to mine host, we passed along the busy High Street, Fargate and Pinstone Lane, then turned down Union Street, where my guests greatly admired the fine erections now being built in that area.

Leaving the town, we proceeded down South Street, as the road down the Sheffield moor is called, passing on our right the old Angel Inn, and noticing as we walked down the road, that many houses are now in the course of erection.

Crossing the bridge over the Porter Brook at the bottom of South Street I pointed out to Mr. and Mrs. Williams the Saw Mill, where in the evenings, two men are usually available to escort persons on foot along the footpath to Sharrow Head. This, of course, is necessary owing to the number of footpads which lurk in this area, ready to pounce on some tired and unsuspecting traveller.

On the left, just before reaching Little Sheffield, we admire the pretty cottage with the large pear tree in the front garden, and I informed my friends, this latter, when full of fruit, is a great source of temptation to the neighbouring youths.

After walking through Little Sheffield past many little cottages, we proceeded along Broom Field, where we found to our dismay, that all the country towards High Field, had been staked out for allotments, probably later to be sold for building. There are, at the present time, only a few cottages in this vicinity.

Reaching the High Field, my friends remarked upon the large expanse of meadow there and Mrs. Williams was charmed by the large residence of Mount Pleasant near the bottom of Sharrow Lane.

A few yards further on we found a cottage set in a delightful garden, where we could rest and take refreshment, meanwhile feasting our eyes on the prospect before us. Just below the garden gate, the road on which we had travelled from town divided, the right hand branch leading by Totley and Dore to Bakewell and the left to Chesterfield by way of Heeley.

We decided that after taking our rest we should take the latter road and this we did, passing on the right the Low Field and its farmhouse, arriving shortly at Heeley Bridge. Pausing on the old bridge, which was first erected in 1567, we watched the little Sheaf, a pleasant river, that owing to the lack of rain during the preceding month, was running very low. I warned my friends not to be deceived by this trickle of water, as I had many times seen the Sheaf in flood and much damage has been caused when it has overflowed its banks.

However, time was passing and we still had much to see, so continuing our perambulations, we walked onwards and found ourselves in Derbyshire.

By a large water wheel called Heeley Mill, we turned right and entered a field path and now indeed began to feel amongst the beauties of our ramble. This pathway, following the river, next led us passed the Little London Tilt and then winding round, it brought us to what is locally called Smithy Wood Bottom. Here were no less than three water wheels at the side of a large expanse of water and Mr. Williams remarked on the ponderous movements of the ancient grinding machinery.

The vicinity of this dam is noted for its beauty and on this fine autumnal day, with the sun breaking through the light fleecy clouds, all the scenery around us was broken into the softest masses, making our feelings calm and serene, harmonizing them with earth and sky.

Looking down the Abbey dale we counted many shades of green, with here and there, the roofs of some fine houses just to be seen amongst the trees.

A little further along this delightful pathway, I pointed out to my companions the little St. Anne's (or Anna's) Well, and whilst we refreshed ourselves with a drink of the sparkling, cold water, I told them, in verse, the legend of this small well:—

Anna's Well

The Vale of Beauchief is a pleasant vale!
And intergacent miles of loveliest scenery,
Betwixt our good old town and that sweet spot,
Repay a summer wanderer for his walk.

Reader, hast thou ne'er pass'd by Heeley Mill,
Along the cool dam side, and onward still
By the deep bottom of Smithy Wood?

Yea, surely so,—if, to delight thine eye,
Sweet walk or lovely prospect may avail,
Or sounds can charm thine ear.

Then would'st thou mark,
Beside the path, that runs embower'd along
The margin of the wood,—a little well,
Transparent, and unrippled by its spring,
The water shines beneath its brink scoop'd circular.

The Redbreast and the Blackbird slake them here,
Winter, and Summer, and throughout the year.

Know then, kind reader, on a poet's word,
That this is Anna's Well: nor let the name
Displease thy fancy, nor offend thine ear,
As by my sole arbitrament imposed;
Nor think that rites, and ceremonial due,
Were here neglected when the name was given.

The lovely maid, in voluntary act,
Lav'd her white palms, and sipped the water here,
The water, as in token of assent
Enshrined her image in its bosom bright;
And when the woods were questioned of their will,
'Say, shall this well be Anna's? to my words
Echo, as sponsor, thrice responded "Anna's".'

And I would fain; that here each rambling girl
Should pause awhile; and the bird nesting youth
Forego his search,—and to their jovial fellows
Point out this spot, and as they pass it, say,
There's Anna's Well!

Mrs. Williams showed extreme delight at this charming story and she asked if I would later write down the poem for her, so that after she and her husband returned home, she could read and remember this pleasant interlude.

This I promised to do and continuing our walk, within a few minutes we arrived at Norton Hammer, as the tilt at that place is designated. Here, from the road that passes by, we saw the sweetest prospect imaginable, a vista of perspective to the westward of us that included a most interesting view of Banner Cross. The light fretted turrets rose from amongst the trees, while nearby we could see the roof and belfrey of the adjacent Ecclesall Chapel.

We then proceeded up the hill beyond and after a strenuous climb reached the summit, where we rested, meanwhile turning about to view the scenery we had just left. Now, from this height, we could see the tower of St. George's Church rising gracefully in the distance, this being backed by the magnificently wooded hill of Wincobank, while nearer our imaginations rested on the spot:—

'Where, mid hill and dale and wood,
Sheffield in the valley stood.'

Our walk at length brought us to Woodseats, where, on turning right up a narrow lane, we passed a picturesque old farmhouse.

About half a mile further on the Chesterfield road I was able to point out to Mr. and Mrs. Williams, the little cottage where very recently Peter Raeney had died. Peter, I explained to my friends, was a young man who was driven insane because his girl, Mary Jones, married another man in Sheffield, on the very day she had promised to marry Peter at Dronfield Church.

The shock to the poor young man was so great and his heart was so troubled, that he immediately took to his bed, which was situated in the rafters of this little cottage. There he stayed, in that cramped space, his legs doubled up under his chin, refusing to leave his bed, until his poor body became malformed and it was impossible for him to straighten out. Eventually, in this sorry state, he died!

My story of this poor man, visibly affected Mrs. Williams and I discreetly looked away, as she wiped a tear from her eyes. I therefore hastened to speak of something more cheerful and the opportunity arose, when a little further on we saw, again on our right hand side, the farm house of Jonathon Booth.

In this ancient farm house, I explained to my companions, had lived Jonathon Booth, a gentleman who had a daughter who was ill in an uncommon manner, in the fact that she had fits of alternative raving, praying, ecstasy and moping. These fits troubled the poor girl for many years until, miraculously, they completely ceased. On the 5th of June, 1753, Wesley, the noted preacher, travelling through Sheffield, heard about this interesting phenomenon and he visited this old farm house and spoke to the girl and her father. Later, he preached a sermon here, to a gathering of the Woodseats people.

This story of such a wonderful cure considerably cheered Mrs. Williams and banished the horror of the former tale from her mind. We then continued with our perambulations and turning right off the Chesterfield road, we entered Beauchief Lane.

How far this lane may be fordable in winter, I know not; but even in this season, we found it in a miry state. It seemed the lane had been suffered to remain unmolested in its original foundation, ever since it was perambulated by the monks of Beauchief, to view their estates at 'Wodesetes'.

After traversing this lane for about a mile, we arrived at the Abbey, a building rather more venerable in association with its history in other days, than imposing in its present appearance.

We rambled about with peculiar emotions amidst the few remaining fragments of this once considerable monastic pile and I remarked that the monastery had mostly perished, as the works of men are continually doing.

But, I exclaimed, amidst assent from Mr. Williams and his dear wife, the hills remain, the River Sheaf runs merrily through the meadows and the green fields and wooded eminences still attest the wondrous beauty of Beauchief and the Abbey Dale.

A Story of Old Sheffield

Based on an article published by Leader and Sons in 1866

Michael Lee was the master of a tool works that occupied a site on a croft near Castle Hill, now entirely covered by the large modern Castle Market. Master Lee, as he was known to his employees, had a son, Godfrey, and a daughter, Judith. The Lee family were very reserved, in fact the old man, Michael, who it is said, had a hideous face, was intensely disliked by all the Sheffield people who knew him. Judith, though an unusually tall and handsome girl, seemed to have the same temperament as her father, but Godfrey was of a different character, pleasant and willing to help whom he could.

Strange stories were told amongst the townsfolk about Master Lee's tool works, how none of the tools, mostly agricultural, had names, just numbers; how these tools were loaded on to pack horses which left at night and travelling by the light of the moon, made for a seaport on the west coast. How, ten days or so later, the pack horses returned, carrying casks which contained sugar and other foreign produce, to be sold later at Sheffield Market.

Children, though frightened of Master Lee, would out of sheer bravado, climb the walls of the tool works in the evening and knock nails into the casks, hoping to make a hole big enough to allow the contents to escape. But, one particular evening, one of the casks broke open and the horrified children saw protruding through the gap, a black hand and arm.

Running home they fetched their parents, who upon investigation found the contents of the cask to be a negro, who judging by the marks upon his body, had been cruelly flogged to death.

The word went round the town like wildfire, obviously the tools made at Master Lee's were for the slave plantations of America, and the anger of the people grew to alarming proportions.

That evening a large mob stormed the works, breaking the gates, sheds, and every other object that they found within reach of their hammers and axes. Then all the tools and anything portable were picked up and dumped in the River Don and Master Lee's works, as such, ceased to exist.

The following day the Lee family left Sheffield and went to live in an isolated farm cottage on the moors near Dore. Here, except for the servants and an occasional farmer, the family saw no one and Master Lee and Judith became more indrawn than ever.

Godfrey however, could not bear living on the wild moorlands and he eventually persuaded his father to allow him to live at Abbeydale, and work a mill, which had been in use since the time when it ground corn for the monks at Beauchief Abbey.

One day Godfrey was on his way to Sheffield town, walking along the old pack horse road from Abbeydale, which passed along what is now Kenwood and came out in Sharrow Lane and so down to town. Turning through the trees into Sharrow Lane, Godfrey saw a pretty teenage girl being assaulted by three youths and he instantly ran to her rescue. Being quite a well built and strong young man, Godfrey soon had the upper hand and within minutes all three youths were lying in the ditch.

Escorting the girl to town, Godfrey discovered her name was Patience Westdale, and that her father was Obadiah Westdale, a Puritan stalwart of Sheffield. This gentleman was very proud of the fact that his great grandfather had fought alongside Colonel Bright of Carbrook Hall, in the Civil Wars.

To Godfrey and Patience it was love at first sight, but when Godfrey asked Obadiah if he could pay court to his daughter, he was met with an instant rebuff and Patience was forbidden to see the young man again.

Meanwhile, the year being 1745, the Young Pretender, Charles Edward, had landed in Scotland and this crisis caused the country to be scoured for soldiers. This brought into the area an officer called Captain Monkton, who passing the Lee homestead at Dore, called at the farmhouse and demanded food for himself and his troops.

Captain Monkton, who always had an eye for the ladies, was struck by the proud handsome beauty of Judith Lee and in the short time he was at the farm cottage he seduced the girl, promising his hand in marriage after the rebellion was over.

For Godfrey and Petience the days and weeks passed slowly. Each Sunday Godfrey would go to Nether Chapel just to get a glimpse of Patience sitting with her father, but of course, they were not allowed to speak a word. Eventually, however, Godfrey managed to get a message to his sweetheart and sometimes they managed to meet in the grove of oaks that surrounded Broomhall Spring. This little wooded beauty spot was situated where Wilkinson Street and Gell Street are today. The pair were so much in love that Godfrey again decided to brave the wrath of Patience's father, but old Obadiah was adamant, refusing to let them marry and telling Godfrey that he must not attempt to see his daughter again.

In December of that year, Prince Charles Edward began his retreat from Derby and Captain Monkton found himself attached to the small army of retreating Scots. Calling again on Judith Lee, the gallant captain realised he had now little interest in the girl and he left almost immediately, promising to return as soon as possible.

Did Judith suspect that her soldier was deserting her? We can only guess.

However, three days after Captain Monkton had departed, servants at the Lee household, going to fetch water from the pond near the house, stumbled upon the body of old Michael Lee. Lying partly covered by the snow that was still falling, the body was a grisly sight.

The servants immediately aroused Godfrey and Judith and as both had appeared to be sleeping soundly, it appeared that Michael had been attacked by someone, perhaps a footpad, prowling about near the farm cottage.

Godfrey despatched a servant to Sheffield to fetch a Minister of Justice, but before this worthy person arrived, a party of soldiers passing by called at the cottage and when told of the crime that had been committed, they decided to investigate. The officer in charge of the troop examined the body and found a number of stab wounds, obviously caused by blows from a sharp knife. He also discovered indistinct footmarks in the snow leading back to the cottage. The officer ordered his men to search the house and in Godfrey's room, a blood stained clasp knife was found, also damp and muddy boots splashed with blood. Upon Godfrey's admission that these articles were his, he was immediately taken prisoner, being charged with the murder of his father.

While awaiting to be tried at Derby Assizes, Godfrey was kept at Hathersage Hall and here Patience and her father were allowed to visit him. Old Obadiah, though still strong in his dislike of the Lee family, could not believe that Godfrey was guilty of the crime of murder and promised his daughter he would do all in his power to help the young man.

When the trial at Derby took place, everything seemed against Godfrey, all the evidence pointing to his guilt. To make matters worse, when Judith was called to give evidence for the defence, she swooned and did not revive sufficiently to be able to make any cohesive statement.

Needless to say, Godfrey was found guilty and sentenced to the gallows.

After the trial Judith returned to Dore, hoping to find a letter from her lover, but neither letter nor the gallant captain were at the cottage. The angry Judith saddled her horse and set out to find Captain Monkton and eventually she overtook him at Carlisle. With fellow officers, Monkton was having a meal when a message was handed to him informing him of Judith's arrival. He sent a reply that he had no wish to see her again, but Judith forced her way into the room and accusing him of playing her false, she informed him she was going to her doom, but that she would take him with her! With this ominous threat and hatred in her heart, Judith returned to Dore, vowing to get her revenge on the unfaithful Captain Monkton.

Meanwhile in the condemned cell at Derby prison, old Obadiah Westdale was saying goodbye to Godfrey, regretting that his efforts to help him had been in vain. Patience was at their lodgings in Derby, too overwrought to set foot outside the house.

On the day set for the hanging, crowds began to gather even before dawn, all in eager anticipation of an entertaining spectacle. From all directions people poured into the area surrounding the gallows, all anxious to witness the last few minutes of the murderer of Michael Lee.

However, when mid-day arrived and there was still no sign of the prisoner being brought from the jail, angry mutterings arose from the mob, which grew in violence when they heard that Godfrey had escaped from the condemned cell and there would be no public hanging that day.

Two days later a wandering packman, or pedlar, arrived at the lodgings of the Westdales and the joy of Patience can be imagined, when the packman turned out to be none other than Godfrey Lee. To Patience and her father, Godfrey explained how, with the help of a friendly warder who believed in his innocence, he had escaped from Derby Gaol. How he had taken to the disguise of a packman, selling small wares, to wander about the streets of the town until he had discovered where the Westdales were lodging. He informed Patience she had no need to worry about him as he had found a good hiding place, where he would be safe until he could prove his innocence.

After Godfrey had left, the Westdales returned to Sheffield, much lighter in heart and hoping they would be able to discover evidence that would clear Godfrey's name.

This evidence was to come much sooner than they expected, for Judith Lee, her soul now twisted with hate, decided to get her revenge on Monkton by giving herself up and denouncing the Captain as the plotter and instigator of the murder of her father. Going to the Constable's Office she wrote out a full confession, stating that her brother Godfrey had tried to stop her relationship with Captain Monkton and, to bring about her brother's ruin, she and Monkton arranged to murder her father, the blame to fall upon Godfrey. She also produced a letter supposedly from Monkton incriminating himself in the plot.

Later, however, at the trial of Judith Lee, the letter was proved to be a forgery and the packed court listened with horror to Judith's confession of how she killed her father, stabbing him many times with Godfrey's clasp knife.

Judith, no longer the proud, handsome girl of former years, was sentenced to death and upon the day of the execution, a greater crowd than ever assembled round the gallows. As Judith mounted the scaffold, the sky darkened and a fierce thunderstorm broke out, thunder and lightning following in quick succession. It grew so dark that the small group of people on the gallows platform could only be seen during the brief flashes of lighning and the crowd grew silent as the hangman adjusted the rope.

Suddenly, a terrific flash, greater than before, lit up the awful scene and the mob gasped to see what appeared to be the disappearance of the victim before their eyes. Then with the next flash they saw the hangman bending over a burnt bundle of clothing. All that was left of Judith Lee was a scorched, blackened corpse!

The great mob of people, that had arrived anticipating an entertaining spectacle, dispersed in terror, hurrying to their homes horrified at the awful intervention of God.

Our story ends on a happier note, for Godfrey Lee received a free pardon and returning to Dore, he lived for a time in the cottage on the moors. Later he took up residence in the mill at Abbeydale and once again he visited Obadiah Westdale to ask for his daughter's hand. Again the old man refused, but Patience, on her knees, eventually persuaded her father that her only happiness lay in marrying Godfrey, and Obadiah gave his blessing.

The couple would have liked to have been married at Nether Chapel, but the law at that time still required that Nonconformists and Conformists alike should go to the Mother Church to be married. So they were married at the Parish Church, now the Cathedral, and enjoyed many happy years of life together.

Ancient Epitaphs

The practice very prevalent today of 'tidying up' our churchyards has robbed us of many interesting and amusing epitaphs which were common on the gravestones in ancient times.

The following brief selection are examples that existed in the churchyards of Sheffield.

In the Parish Churchyard a stone in memory of Richard Walker, of the Royal Regiment of Horse Guards, who died on 22nd June, 1800, stated:

'Within this dark and silent grave
Here lies a soldier just and brave;
And when the awful trump shall sound
He is for settled quarters bound.'

In the same churchyard, on the stone of Sarah Oliver, who died in 1818, aged 30, was an epitaph that could be read two ways:

'She was——
But words are wanting to say what,
Think what a wife should be——
She was that!'

Not an epitaph, but a pathetic inscription was on a stone 'To the Memory of Aaron Nichells who departed this life, April 20th, 1810. Aged 63 years. Also Catherine, his wife, who departed this life on the same day. Aged 63.

The bursting of grinding wheels cost many lives in the grinding hulls of old Sheffield and an incident of this type caused the death of William Hobson in 1815, whose gravestone bore the epitaph:

'Beneath this stone a grinder lies,
A sudden death ath close his eyes;
He lost his life by the breaking of a stone,
We hope his soul to Heaven has gone.'

In Beauchief Abbey Churchyard a stone of 1758 tells of a gamekeeper who accidently shot himself.

'A Game keeper I was at Beauchief Hall,
At Dore my fatal gun caused me to fall,
Which made a speedy passage through my head
And sent me to the mansions of the dead.
Repent in time, consider mortal man,
Thy race extends no further than a span,
Man is like a flower that's in the morning blown,
Then before the night, is withered and cut down.

Another stone in the same churchyard, dated 1801, has the inscription:

'She was a wife loving and kind,
And to her husband always bore a virtuous mind
Even unto the very last,
I hope to the Lord, in heaven she's cast.'

Finally, in St. Philip's Churchyard, on a stone to the memory of John Kidd, who died in 1844:

'Here lies the body of John Kidd,
In eternal realms his soul is hid.
A railway engine did him kill
And crush-ed his poor head so ill!'

Humour in Sheffield History

The lighter side of local history is illustrated in the following anecdotes which came to light during my researches into life in 18th and 19th century Sheffield.

The Lepping Stones and the Parson

The Lepping Stones across the River Don occupied a line about thirty yards below the Crescent Bridge, near the entrance to what is now the Wednesday Football Club ground. Pedestrians wishing to cross the river found it necessary to leap from stone to stone, whilst horse drawn vehicles forded the river on the Middlewood side.

The stepping stones were usually very greasy and many people, attempting to reach the other bank, fell in the water and got a soaking.

One of these unfortunate persons was the Rev. Samuel Danks Waddy, who, on his way to preach at Wadsley Bridge Chapel, while crossing the Lepping Stones, slipped and fell in the river.

It is reported the good parson did not preach a 'dry' sermon on that particular day!

The Doctor and the Parson

One of the most unusual residents at Loxley House was a man called Henry Payne. A rather eccentric medical practitioner, his cure for all the ills of the flesh was simply a very hot blanket!

During the latter part of his life, Doctor Payne quarrelled with the parson in Wadsley and the outcome was he swore he would never enter the church again.

The parson insisted that he would, clinching his argument with the remark, 'You will, when you are carried in head first in your coffin!'

However, the doctor was not to be defeated even in death, for he left orders that he was to be buried on his own estate without a church ceremony.

So when he died, in 1895, two servants carried the coffin to a grave dug in the grounds of Loxley House, lowered the coffin in, and without any kind of religious ceremony, filled in the grave.

Disturbance in the Parish Church

Francis Jessop, Rector of Treeton, the younger son of Francis Jessop of Broom Hall, was one Sunday in the Parish Church listening to a sermon given by the Vicar, a Mr. Drake.

Jessop, disagreeing with something the Vicar said, suddenly jumped up from his seat, levelled a loaded pistol at Mr. Drake and shouted, 'Duck or Drake, I'll have at thee, mallard!'

He would actually have fired at the Vicar if he had not been restrained by his friends. Meanwhile, Mr. Drake had crouched down behind his pulpit and he stayed trembling below until he was informed that Mr. Jessop had been taken from the church!

The First Umbrella

Many amusing comments were made about the first people to carry umbrellas in our city.

The honour of being the first person to use such a device has been claimed for at least four people, these being: Mr. Holy of Holy Green, Mr. Greaves, Mr. Newbould and William Trickett.

The latter was Master Cutler in 1771, and when he first appeared carrying an umbrella, his brother Enoch joined in the general laughter, with the remark, 'See thee, our Bill's getten a walkin' stick wi' petticoats on!'

Duck Power

In 1854 a man called Harvey Teesdale floated down the River Don from West Bar, in a basket pulled along by a number of ducks!

Horse Power

Up to 1911 a one horse bus ran from Dore and Totley Station to Totley. It was driven by a little old man called Jimmy Larder. The nearest Jimmy had ever been to Sheffield was once when he visited Millhouses.

It is said that he used to shout and crack his whip loudly, but the old horse just ignored him and trotted on at its own slow pace!

Lucy the Pig

Situated in West Bar, near the corner of Corporation Street, was the Gaiety Music Hall, run by a German called Metzler. This gentleman had also a pork shop and a public house nearby.

Mr. Metzler had a tame pig called Lucy that was very fond of beer. A customer gave it two quarts one day and the pig went under a table and lay very still.

Mr. Metzler came in, looked at it and in a tone of disgust said, 'Lucy's as drunk as a pig!'

The Pigs and the Pinder

Pinfold Street acquires its name from the 'pinfold' or 'pound' that existed on the south side of the lane as early as 1592. The latest one survived until 1835, when it was demolished to make way for street widening.

The 'Pinder' was the man in charge of the pinfold, a person extremely disliked and regarded as the common foe.

In the old days the community combined to hire a swineherd to look after their pigs. He would take the pigs to common land outside the little town. When the swineherd sounded his horn, pigs would rush from every direction, from houses, shops, grinding wheels and 'swyne howles' (pig sties). They would rush down entries and gennels with joyous grunts.

Later it became the habit to allow the pigs to roam the streets, grubbing among the refuse which was very abundant.

Near Christmas, many a working man's family were put on

short rations, the food saved being used to fatten the pigs. Troughs were situated at the doors of most of the houses in the town and the pigs would feed on the public footpath.

The pigs were summoned by their owners rattling the pig trough and it was amazing how they would rush to heed the call.

This annoyed the Pinder exceedingly, for when he was trying to run a wandering pig into the pinfold and so claim four pence for its return, the owner would set up a great clattering and the pig would escape, to be safely housed before the Pinder could catch up with it!

The Stupid Club

The Stupid Club was a Sick and Dividing Club, more sick than dividing! It met in the old Blue Bell Inn in Worksop Road, Attercliffe, in the 1880's. The members would meet to argue on any topic and they usually ended in fighting.

The funds of the club were divided mainly in the form of liquid refreshment, the sick money never being drawn because of a rule that said a member had to give a fortnight's notice before being ill!

The Chairman was called the Spill Major, he sat nearest the fire and when a member required a light for his pipe, the Major lighted a paper spill and passed it to him.

The Spill Major was also supposed to keep the members in order, but when he tried they would not listen. They were too stupid!

Johannaites. (Johanna's Secret Box of Writings)

In 1824 there existed a chapel in Coal Pit Lane (now Cambridge Street) that had belonged to the religious sect called Johannaites. These people were followers of a lady called Johanna Southcott who, it was expected, would give birth to a new Messiah!

One devoted follower who lived on the east side of Nursery Street, near the Wicker end, had a beautiful cradle made to hold the baby Messiah.

Unfortunately, on December 27th, 1814, Johanna died, at the age of 60, still undelivered!

A Few Notes on Parts 2 and 3

Fish in the Don. John Harrison in his survey of 1637 writes, 'The chiefest ffishinge within the manno is the rivers that passeth through the same wherein are a great store of salmons, trouts, chevens (chubs), eeles, and other small fish.'

Old Sheffield Town Hall. This stood on the south-east corner of the Parish Church yard. (The Parish Church is now the Cathedral) The Town Hall was only a small two-storeyed building, the upper room being used for the town's business and the lower room for the jail. An extract from the Town Trustee's Accounts, made by Vincent Eyre, reads, '1700—paid Mr Renny the first payment towards building the Town Hall—£50.' The Town Stocks were also situated near the Parish Church gates.

Tontine Inn. On 29th September, 1785, it was resolved at a meeting held in Sheffield, to erect a commodious inn on the site 'where the Castle Barns now stand', at a cost of not less than £4,000, this sum to be raised by a tontine. There were 50 subscribers of £100 each, including the Earl of Surrey, who took five shares. Each subscription nominated a life, during the continuance of which he was to receive an equal share of the rents and profits.

The Tontine was a great posting or coaching house and there were always twenty horses and five post boys ready when the yard bell rang and the call given 'First pair out!'

At one time the host had as many as 300 horses standing at different staging posts. However, when the railways arrived the whole posting establishment collapsed and all the horses were sold, no matter what the price.

In 1890, the Duke of Norfolk purchased the Tontine Inn for £7,720 so that he could demolish it to erect the Norfolk Market Hall on the site. Woolco's large store now stands upon the spot where the famous coaching inn was erected at the corner of Haymarket and Dixon Lane.

Origin of old Sheffield Saying. 'Till mor ship lands at t'bottom o' Park Hill' obviously derived from the days of the merchant adventurers, whose common remark was, 'Wait until my ship comes in!'

Punishment in the Eighteenth Century. Hanging was the usual punishment for the crime of stealing. A person could also be hanged for picking pockets, if more than one shilling (5p) was taken! It was also a hanging matter for stealing goods worth more than five shillings from a shop. In Sheffield it was a common occurrence, as a minor punishment, to be put in a cart and whipped on the bare shoulders as the cart proceeded from the Church Gates down to Lady's Bridge.

Sheffield Field Names. Fairbanks recorded many of the ancient field names in the Sheffield area, which included the following: At Tinsley: Swan Nest, Cinquefoil Close, Arcos, Freezeland Close, Plonk Holme and Temple Bank. At Darnall: Bessy Meadow, Fiddle Case, Great Tongue, In the Hades and Pogonore Land. In Attercliffe: Castle Meadow, Goodman Storth, Herring Field, Long Hades, Mountney Field, Mag Field, Partridge Flatt, Slattering Rig, Stacye Field and Lamb Pool (Jansen Street, off Attercliffe Common, was originally called Lamb Pool Lane.) At Dore: Crude Sick, America, Floated Field, Savage Acres, Saint Igna, Wag Wood, Tippy Lands and Maiden's Hillock.

Woodhouse. This village derived its name from the Old English 'Wodehus', meaning a house in a wood. The 'Cross Daggers' is a two storey stone built house of 1658. It is being preserved, along with the Market Cross and Stocks nearby, in the midst of modern development.

Sheffield Park. This large park covered about 2,500 acres and reached from the River Sheaf (near what is now the Sheffield Railway Station), to Gleadless Town End. It was full of magnificent oak trees, mostly cut down in the seventeenth and eighteenth centuries. The Manor Lodge was built in the midst of this park by George, 4th Earl of Shrewsbury, early in the reign of Henry VIII. There was just one private road through the park, with gates at each entrance.

Old Pump, Grimesthorpe. This iron pump was erected in the 19th century to replace a much earlier wooden one.

Bat, Stick and Trip. This refers to the ancient game of 'Peggy', which was rather similar to Knur and Spell. This game was common some forty years ago and the author remembers playing 'Peggy' for many hours when a boy. The 'bat' consisted of a thick stick of wood, the 'stick' was a small piece of wood laid on the ground and the 'trip' was a further short piece sharpened at both ends. The 'trip' was laid partly across the 'stick', the end of the 'trip' was then sharply hit with the 'bat', causing it to spring about three feet into the air. This had then to be hit again as hard as possible. The distance between the batter and where the 'trip' fell had then to be paced out, and naturally, the winner was the person who had hit the 'trip' the longest distance.

Obviously the Methodist minister was pointing out to young Mather that he who played games on a Sunday was 'on the wrong road', 'The road to Loxley Edge' refers to what happened to the murderer, Frank Fern, who was gibbeted on this bleak common.

The Twybells of Southey. The ancient family, of good yeoman stock, is directly connected with the author's family. This happened when William Vickers married Elizabeth Twybell of Southey, in the middle of the 18th century. The author is a direct descendant of William and Elizabeth. From William Vickers' brother John, came Edward Vickers, who became the head of the famous Don Steel Works—Vickers & Company—now part of the British Steel Corporation.

Wadsley Hall. The sticking of pins or bodkins into the mantelpiece by guests, seems to have been a common practice in those days. The reason for this ancient custom is, however, lost in antiquity.

Lepping Stones. The stepping stones or 'Lepping Stones' across the River Don occupied a line about thirty yards below the Crescent Bridge, near the entrance to what is now the Wednesday Football Ground. Pedestrians wishing to cross the river found it necessary to leap from stone to stone, whilst horse-drawn vehicles forded the river on the Middlewood side.

Sir Jeffry Wyatville. This famous architect was born plain Jeffry Wyatt, on the 3rd August, 1766, at Burton on Trent. He eventually became the designer of over 100 buildings, among which are the north wing of Chatsworth House and the entrance and various additions to Longleat. However he is best known for his work on Windsor Castle, started in 1824. For this, King George IV bestowed on him a knighthood, he was allowed to alter his name to Wyatville and he was given a residence in the Winchester Tower. Sir Jeffry died on 10th February, 1940, in London. A portrait of him, painted by Sir Francis Chantrey, is in the National Portrait Gallery.

Abbeydale House. This splendid mansion was completely ruined by the erection of a brick built laundry that occupies the whole of the front grounds and is attached to the front of the house. The house is at present empty and in a very dilapidated state. However it is hoped that restoration work will be carried out in the near future.

The Farm. This was a mansion that was formerly the Sheffield home of the Duke of Norfolk and his agent. It was rebuilt in 1824, the dining room having a ceiling copied from the one in the 'Mary, Queen of Scots Room', at the Manor Lodge. The very fine grounds were spoilt when the Midland Railway was constructed. The mansion has now been demolished!

Bole Hill, Norton. Bole Hill is situated at the top of Cobnar Road, an ancient way still unfit for motor traffic. Bole Hills were places where iron was smelted in open wood furnaces, the tops of the hills being necessary to ensure a good draught. There are Bole Hills at Crookes and other places.

Chipping House. This was a mansion that stood on the site of the present Chippinghouse Road at Abbeydale. Steade Road, Brookfield Road and St Ronan's Road, etc., were laid out on the grounds of Chipping House.

Woodseats. The derivation of this name comes from the Old English 'Wodesettes' or 'Wodesete' meaning a fold in wood.

Little Sheffield. This was (and still is) the area at the end of London Road, near the Moor Foot. Some of the old cottages still exist now converted into shops.

The Use of Rice at Weddings. In olden times it was the custom to throw rice over the bride and bridegroom as a symbol of fertility. Today paper confetti is used for the same purpose.

Ebenezer Elliott's Statue. The bronze statue by Burnard was erected in the Market Place in 1854, six years after Elliott's death. It was removed to Weston Park in 1875 when the roadway was widened.

The Court Leet. The Court Leet or Court of 'Sembly Quest was the people's own court guaranteed to them by Lord Furnival. At the court, minor offences, such as defiling the town wells or failure to scour ditches, were dealt with, the judges and jury being the people themselves.

The Legend of Ringinglow. There appears to be no substance to this story, as Hunter, the historian, tells of a 'pile of stones called Ringinglawe' mentioned in 1559. There is also no record existing of any bequest to the bell ringers of the Parish Church at this time.

Frank Fern's Gibbet. In the year 1783, Frank Fern robbed and murdered a Sheffield jeweller who was passing over Loxley Common. Fern was captured the following day and after his trial he was executed, his body being hung in chains on a gibbet near the scene of his crime.

The King's Head Hotel. This was a very ancient coaching inn, first mentioned in the Burgery Accounts of 1572.

The Angel Inn. This stood at the corner of Button Lane and Backfields and was demolished to make way for Charter Square and the Grosvenor Hotel block of buildings. This inn should not be confused with the more famous hostelry of the same name that existed in Angel Street.

Porter Brook. This is now channelled under the Moorfoot, but a little of it can still be seen at the side of the S & E Cooperative Stores. The saw-mill stood approximately at the junction of Ecclesall Road and The Moor.

Cottage, Moorfoot. This cottage was situated in the centre of what is now St. Mary's Gate and where the Brunswick Chapel of 1834 formerly stood. Little Sheffield was a collection of cottages stretching from the Porter to Hill Street.

Broomfield. This was the name given to what is now London Road, between Little Sheffield and Highfield.

Mount Pleasant. This building can still be seen situated between Sharrow Lane and Sitwell Road. It is now a Community Centre.

Junction of Abbeydale Road and London Road at Highfield. An old milestone which stood at the roadside can still be seen preserved on top of a brick wall next door to the Royal Public House.

Derbyshire Boundary. The Meers Brook, which was formerly the boundary between Yorkshire and Derbyshire, runs in a culvert under the roadway a short distance above Albert Road. The Heeley Toll Bar was situated immediately over this boundary brook.

Heeley Mill. Heeley Mill and Water Wheel were situated near the footbridge from Saxon Road which crosses the Sheaf to Broadfield Road. Heeley Mill existed before the year 1600.

Little London Tilt. This stood near Broadfield Road, at the end of the footpath from Little London Road. At Smithy Wood three water wheels were in use, one for tripping the hammer, one for driving the blowers and one for operating the grinding wheel. These water wheels were in existence in 1496. One wheel still remained, in a ruined state, in the 1930's. The large dam is now filled in and works have been built on the site. Smithy Wood extended from the dam up the hillside to Scarsdale Top.

St Anne's Well. This little well, like the dam and wheels, has completely disappeared.

Norton Hammer. The tilt hammer known as Norton Hammer is no more, but a few old cottages remain to remind us of the Waterwheels and works that existed there as long ago as 1560. The future of these cottages is uncertain.

The Dale Farm. A narrow lane, The Dale, is still in existence, but the Dale Farm, where Gillot of Steel Pen Nib fame was born, was demolished in

1965. The joists and beams of the old farmhouse were solid rough-hewn oak tree trunks and the walls were of stone two feet thick. A modern factory now stands on this site.

Peter Raeney's Cottage. This would be somewhere near the site of the present Big Tree Hotel.

Jonathon Booth's House. This was situated down a small lane opposite the bottom of Cobnar Road.

Beauchief Lane. Now the very pleasant Abbey Lane.

Beauchief and the Abbey Dale. A considerable amount of beauty still remains in this area. Luckily this vicinity includes Millhouses Park, Beauchief Gardens and the extensive Ecclesall Woods.

Broomhall Spring. This was originally a spring of water in the centre of a pleasant grove of trees. After the houses were built in this area, a stone with the inscription 'Spring Garden Well' was to be seen in the garden of a house at the corner of Gell Street and Conway Street. This has long since disappeared.

Blue Bell Inn. The building is still in existence, but the old public house has now become a warehouse.

Johannaites. This religious sect must still exist as an advertisement appears infrequently in the Press which states that 'the troubles of this world will not cease until the Bishops open Johanna's Secret Box of Writings!'

INDEX